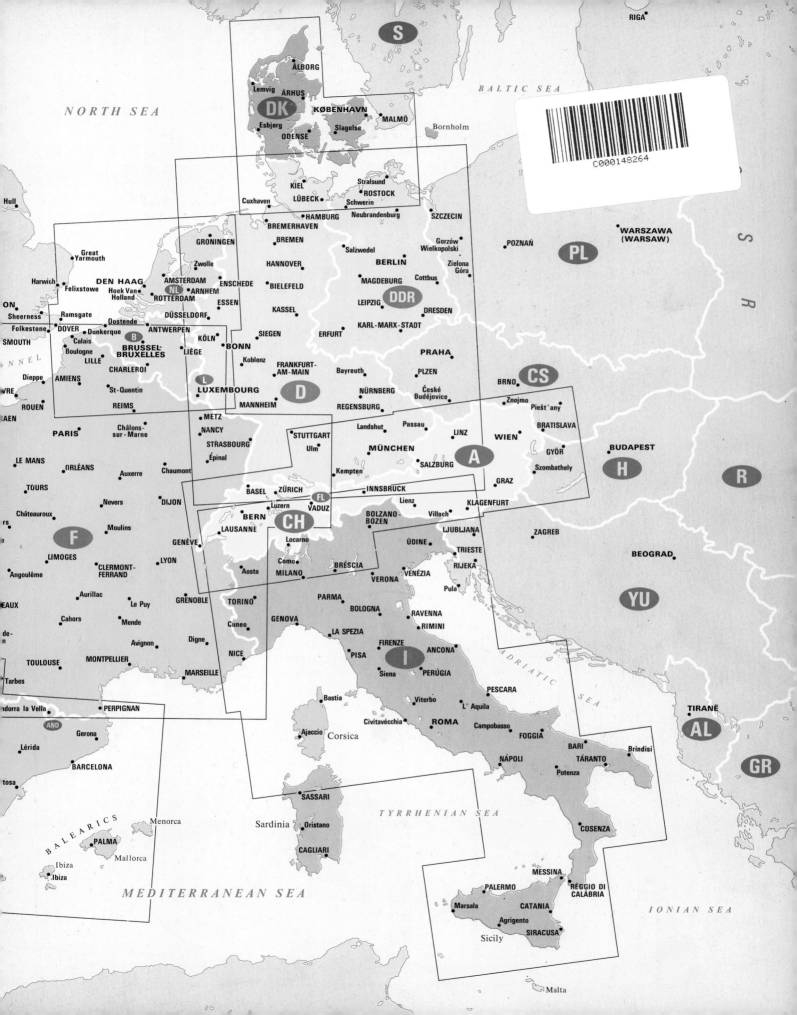

The contents of this publication are believed correct at the time of printing. Nevertheless the AA can accept no responsibility for errors or omissions, or for changes in the details given.

Produced by the Cartographic Department of the Publications Division of The Automobile Association.

Photographic sources: Austrian National Tourist Office; Belgian National Tourist Office; Danish Tourist Board; French Government Tourist Office; German National Tourist Office; Italian State Tourist Office; Luxembourg National Tourist Office; Netherlands National Tourist Office; Portuguese National Tourist Office; Susan Griggs Photographic Agency; Swiss National Tourist Office.

Phototypeset, printed and bound by Purnell & Sons Ltd, Paulton, Avon.

Published by The Automobile Association, Fanum House, Basingstoke, Hampshire RG21 2EA.

© The Automobile Association 1980
ISBN 0 86145 029 9   55945

MOTORISTS' ATLAS OF WESTERN EUROPE

CONTENTS

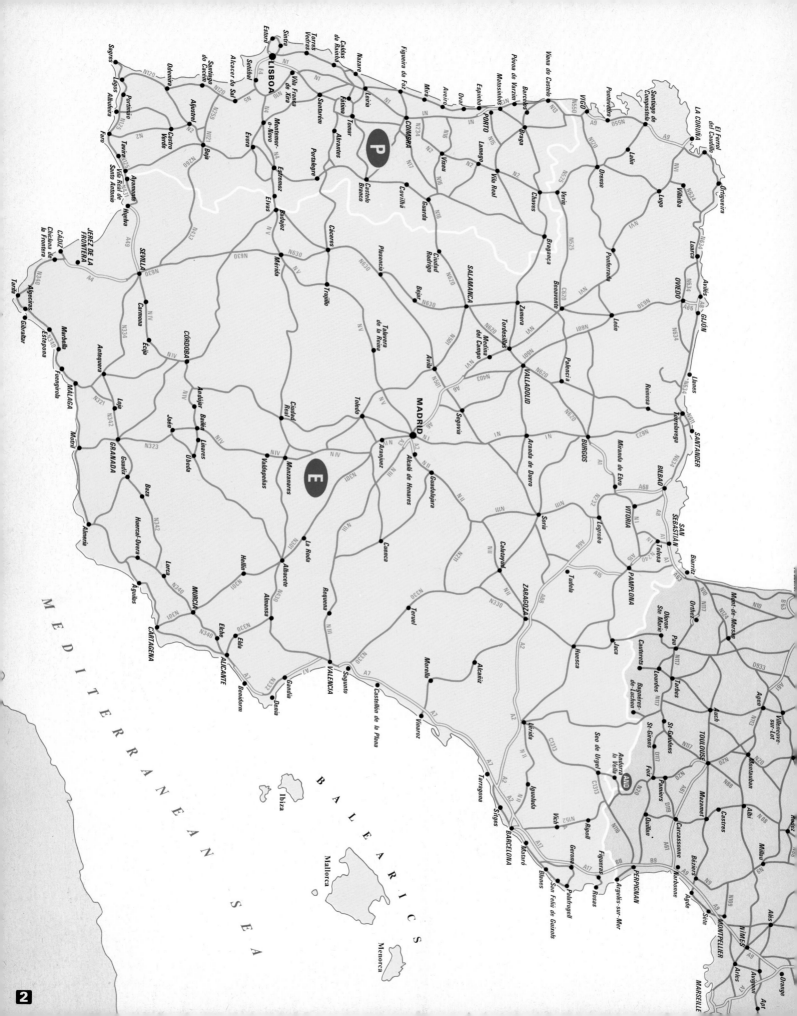

ROUTES ACROSS EUROPE

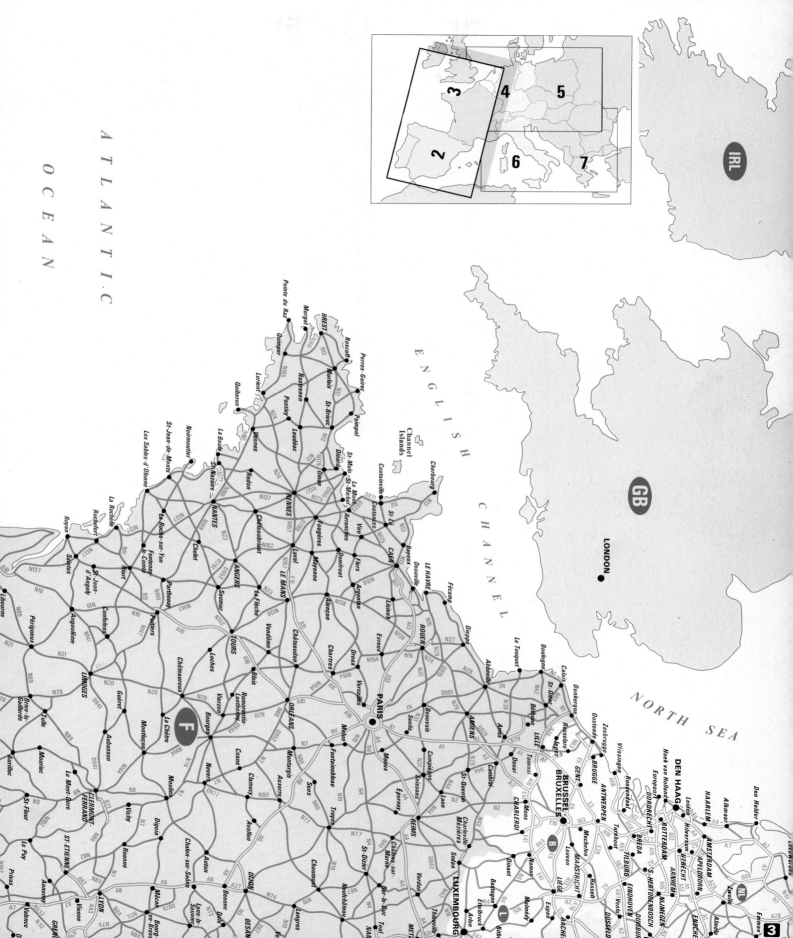

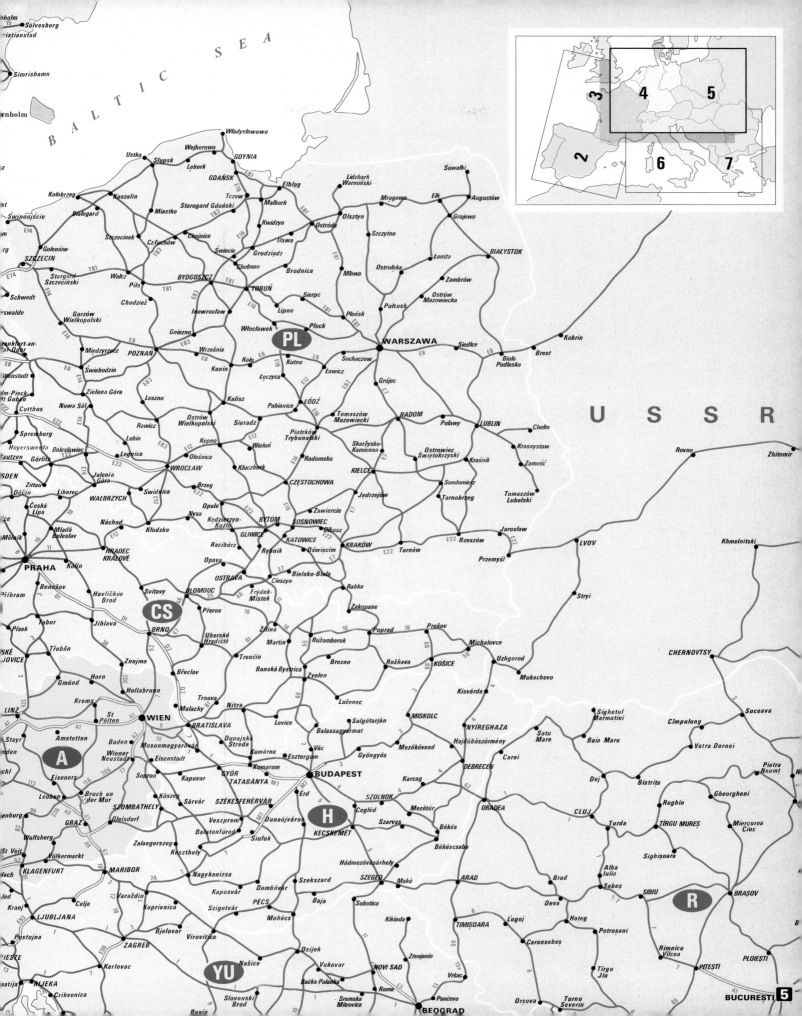

LEGEND

MOTORWAY AUTOROUTE AUTOBAHN AUTOSTRADA

A4	Dual Carriageway	Double chaussée
	Getrennte Fahrbahnen	Carreggiate separate
A7	Single Carriageway	Une seule chaussée
	Eine Fahrbahn (Autostrasse)	Carreggiata unica

TOLL MOTORWAY AUTOROUTE À PÉAGE
GEBÜHRENPFLICHTIGE AUTOBAHN AUTOSTRADA A PEDAGGIO

A1	Dual Carriageway	Double chaussée
	Getrennte Fahrbahnen	Carreggiate separate
A6	Single Carriageway	Une seule chaussée
	Eine Fahrbahn (Autostrasse)	Carreggiata unica

MOTORWAY JUNCTIONS ÉCHANGEUR AUTOROUTE
AUTOBAHN ANSCHLUSS STAZIONE CON SVINCOLI

Restricted access (Colour indicates entry or exit)	
Accès restreint (la zone de couleur indique l'entrée ou la sortie)	
Beschränkte Auf oder Abfahrt (das farbige Feld zeigt die mögliche Auf oder Abfahrt an)	
Accesso ristretto (ingresso od usita indicati a colori)	
No restriction	Sans restriction
Keine Beschränkung	Nessuna restrizione
Service area	Aire de service
Tankstelle mit Raststätte	Area di servizio
Under Construction	En construction
Im Bau	In costruzione

ROADS ROUTES STRASSEN STRADE

	Primary route	Route primaire
	Hauptverbindungsstrasse	Rotta primaria
	Main road	Route principle
	Hauptstrasse	Strade principale
	Secondary road	Route secondaire
	Nebenstrasse	Strade secondarie
	Other road	Autre route
	Sonstige Strasse	Altre strade
D59 E57 N24	Road numbers	Numéros de route
	Strassennummern	Numeri delle strade
	Dual Carriageway or four lanes	Chaussées séparées ou quatre voies
	Getrennte Fahrbahnen oder 4 Fahrspuren	Carreggiate separate / 4 corsie
	Under Construction	En construction
	Im Bau	In costruzione
Toll / TOLL	Toll road	Route à péage
	Gebührenpflichtige Strasse	Strada a pedaggio
	Transit route (GDR)	Route de transit (RDA)
	Transitstrasse (DDR)	Via di transito (RDT)

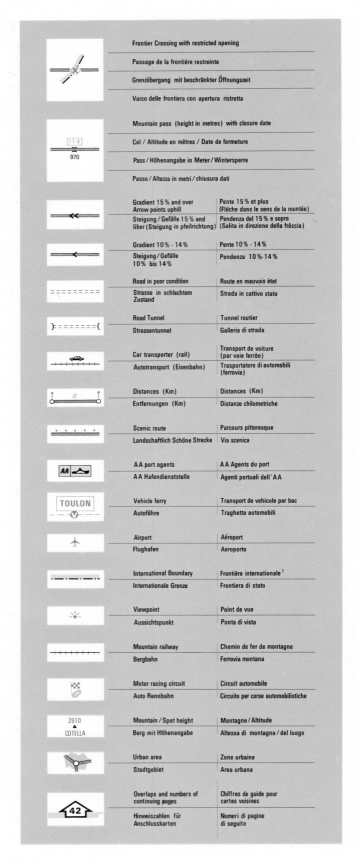

	Frontier Crossing with restricted opening	
	Passage de la frontière restreinte	
	Grenzübergang mit beschränkter Öffnungszeit	
	Varco delle frontiera con apertura ristretta	
11·4 / 970	Mountain pass (height in metres) with closure date	
	Col / Altitude en mètres / Date de fermeture	
	Pass / Höhenangabe in Meter / Wintersperre	
	Passo / Altezza in metri / chiusura dati	
	Gradient 15% and over Arrow points uphill	Pente 15% et plus (Flèche dans le sens de la montée)
	Steigung / Gefälle 15% and über (Steigung in pfeilrichtung)	Pendenza del 15% e sopra (Salita in direzione della fréccia)
	Gradient 10% - 14%	Pente 10% - 14%
	Steigung / Gefälle 10% bis 14%	Pendenza 10%-14%
	Road in poor condition	Route en mauvais état
	Strasse in schlechtem Zustand	Strada in cattivo stato
	Road Tunnel	Tunnel routier
	Strassentunnel	Galleria di strada
	Car transporter (rail)	Transport de voiture (par voie ferrée)
	Autotransport (Eisenbahn)	Trasportatore di automobili (ferrovia)
8	Distances (Km)	Distances (Km)
	Entfernungen (Km)	Distanze chilometriche
	Scenic route	Parcours pittoresque
	Landschaftlich Schöne Strecke	Via scenica
AA	A A port agents	A A Agents du port
	A A Hafendienststelle	Agenti portuali dell'AA
TOULON V	Vehicle ferry	Transport de vehicule par bac
	Autofähre	Traghetto automobili
✈	Airport	Aéroport
	Flughafen	Aeroporto
	International Boundary	Frontière internationale[1]
	Internationale Grenze	Frontiera di stato
	Viewpoint	Point de vue
	Aussichtspunkt	Punta di vista
	Mountain railway	Chemin de fer de montagne
	Bergbahn	Ferrovia montana
	Motor racing circuit	Circuit automobile
	Auto Rennbahn	Circuito per corse automobilistiche
2910 ▲ COTELLA	Mountain / Spot height	Montagne / Altitude
	Berg mit Höhenangabe	Altezza di montagna / del luogo
	Urban area	Zone urbaine
	Stadtgebiet	Area urbana
42	Overlaps and numbers of continuing pages	Chiffres de guide pour cartes voisines
	Hinweiszahlen für Anschlusskarten	Numeri di pagine di seguito

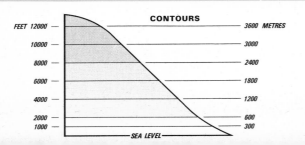

CONTOURS

FEET 12000	3600 METRES
10000	3000
8000	2400
6000	1800
4000	1200
2000	600
1000	300
SEA LEVEL	

SCALE 1: 1000 000 or 16 miles to 1 inch (approx)

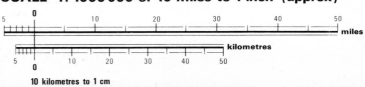

10 kilometres to 1 cm

DESTINATIONS

(in miles from major ports)

CALAIS

Athens	1927
Barcelona	865
Basle	480
Belgrade	1216
Berlin	574
Biarritz	653
Brindisi	1315
Brussels	122
Cologne	253
Florence	881
Frankfurt	371
Geneva	506
Genoa	741
Hamburg	475
Innsbruck	684
Lisbon	1305
Luxembourg	256
Lyon	469
Madrid	981
Marseilles	664
Milan	700
Munich	614
Naples	1184
Nice	761
Paris	182
Prague	687
Rome	1053
Salzburg	700
Strasbourg	387
Trieste	884
Turin	661
Venice	857
Vienna	820

OSTEND

Athens	1876
Barcelona	869
Basle	433
Belgrade	1165
Berlin	523
Biarritz	656
Brindisi	1290
Brussels	71
Cologne	202
Florence	856
Frankfurt	320
Geneva	509
Genoa	750
Hamburg	424
Innsbruck	633
Lisbon	1308
Luxembourg	204
Lyon	472
Madrid	984
Marseilles	667
Milan	668
Munich	563
Naples	1159
Nice	764
Paris	196
Prague	636
Rome	1028
Salzburg	649
Strasbourg	336
Trieste	833
Turin	666
Venice	832
Vienna	769

CHERBOURG

Athens	2057
Barcelona	782
Basle	532
Belgrade	1346
Berlin	820
Biarritz	515
Brindisi	1363
Brussels	359
Cologne	470
Florence	929
Frankfurt	588
Geneva	543
Genoa	779
Hamburg	732
Innsbruck	768
Lisbon	1167
Luxembourg	421
Lyon	506
Madrid	843
Marseilles	701
Milan	742
Munich	744
Naples	1232
Nice	799
Paris	221
Prague	870
Rome	1101
Salzburg	830
Strasbourg	522
Trieste	997
Turin	698
Venice	906
Vienna	995

LE HAVRE

Athens	1960
Barcelona	805
Basle	434
Belgrade	1249
Berlin	705
Biarritz	514
Brindisi	1265
Brussels	244
Cologne	355
Florence	831
Frankfurt	473
Geneva	445
Genoa	682
Hamburg	617
Innsbruck	670
Lisbon	1166
Luxembourg	310
Lyon	408
Madrid	842
Marseilles	603
Milan	644
Munich	647
Naples	1134
Nice	701
Paris	125
Prague	768
Rome	1003
Salzburg	733
Strasbourg	425
Trieste	899
Turin	600
Venice	808
Vienna	896

BOULOGNE

Athens	1942
Barcelona	835
Basle	487
Belgrade	1231
Berlin	598
Biarritz	622
Brindisi	1294
Brussels	146
Cologne	269
Florence	860
Frankfurt	387
Geneva	475
Genoa	712
Hamburg	510
Innsbruck	702
Lisbon	1274
Luxembourg	260
Lyon	438
Madrid	950
Marseilles	633
Milan	673
Munich	630
Naples	1162
Nice	730
Paris	151
Prague	703
Rome	1032
Salzburg	716
Strasbourg	392
Trieste	900
Turin	631
Venice	837
Vienna	835

DIEPPE

Athens	1906
Barcelona	800
Basle	429
Belgrade	1195
Berlin	648
Biarritz	527
Brindisi	1260
Brussels	195
Cologne	306
Florence	826
Frankfurt	424
Geneva	440
Genoa	677
Hamburg	549
Innsbruck	665
Lisbon	1179
Luxembourg	267
Lyon	403
Madrid	855
Marseilles	598
Milan	639
Munich	593
Naples	1129
Nice	696
Paris	120
Prague	708
Rome	998
Salzburg	679
Strasbourg	371
Trieste	894
Turin	613
Venice	803
Vienna	837

SPAIN & PORTUGAL

KEY TO MAP PAGES

SPAIN

Compact mass of land separated from the rest of Europe by the Pyrénées. Spain occupies about six-sevenths of the total area, Portugal the rest. A large part consists of a plâteau of ancient rocks, most over 2,000ft above sea level and known as the Meseta from the Spanish word for a tableland.

Olive trees in the Sierra Nevada

The Meseta

Was uplifted and tilted during the mountain-building movements which formed the Alps. A series of ranges (sierras) was formed across the centre of the plâteau rising to over 8,800ft. The most continuous, the Sierra de Guadarrama lies to the north of Madrid, the

Three distinct climatic types can be distinguished. The Meseta has a somewhat extreme climate, partly because it is separated by ranges from the surrounding seas, particularly from Atlantic influences on the west. Madrid has a dry summer with a mean July temperature of 24°C and daytime figures reaching far higher, while in January frosts and bitter winds are common. The rainfall is only about 16 inches, almost entirely falling in autumn and winter. By contrast the north-west coast has a mild humid climate, the result of its maritime situation, with seasonal temperatures varying from 7° to 18°C. By contrast again the south-east coastlands have a Mediterranean-type climate.

snow-covered crests can be seen from the city. This is the bleakest and least hospitable region.

Two shallow depressions on either side of the central sierras occupy most of the Meseta; to the north is the basin of Old Castile, to the south is New Castile. Old Castile is drained by the Douro, which flows westwards to the Portuguese frontier, the basin of New Castile by the Tagus and the Guadiana.

These basins form great areas of poor lands. On the clay soils in the lower parts wheat is the main crop, with barley in drier districts, occasionally beans and lentils, but yields are low and, as a rule, a cereal crop has to be succeeded by one or more years of fallow during which the surface is kept covered to store several seasons' rainfall.

More than half the surface of the Meseta carries poor pasture which provides winter grazing for large flocks of merino sheep. The arid heat of summer makes it necessary for the animals to move into the uplands; most animals are taken to the Cantabrian mountains or the Sierra Nevada. Beef cattle are reared, including the Iberic fighting bulls.

The Meseta has some importance as a producer of minerals for the rocks in the Sierra Morena have yielded copper since the days of the Phoenicians and variety of ores (mercury, zinc, lead, wolfram) is still mined. Esparto grass is used for making paper, cordage, hats, fans and mats.

The Northern Uplands comprise a) Galicia b) Cantabrian Mountains and c) Pyrénées:

Galicia
Consists of an ancient granite plâteau broken by east-west faults called rias (dissected by river valleys). Similar in character to Brittany and to Cornwall/Devon in relief, coastline, climate and occupations. The main ports are Corunna (La Coruña), Vigo and the naval base of El Ferrol.

A moist climate supports rich pastures and it is an important dairy region; maize, vegetables (especially onions) and fruit (cider-apples) are grown.

Cantabrian Mountains
Form a series of ranges separated by gorgelike valleys—the highest and most rugged parts are the Picos de Europa which fall steeply to a narrow coastal plain, with dairying and the cultivation of maize, vegetables and fruits.

The wealth however lies in the mineral deposits—Spain's chief coalfield near Oviedo produces about 9 million tons each year. Manganese, cobalt, zinc and other ores are mined.

Bilbao, situated 7 miles from the sea is a manufacturing city with general and electrical engineering, manufacture of tyres, ten shipyards and integrated steelworks.

Pyrénées
On the Spanish side the descent from the frontier ridge is more gradual than in France and foothills are crossed by valleys draining to the Ebro. On the slopes in the west rainfall is sufficient for forest, but for the most part the hills are covered with poor pasture or scrub.

Betic Cordillera
In the north it consists of limestone ranges

bordering the Guadalquivar valley, while farther south are the Sierra Nevada. The latter were affected by glaciation, prominent pyramid peaks exceed 11,000ft in height and there are many cirques and lakes.

The southern valleys and basins are well watered and form districts of oasis cultivation growing fruit, vegetables, vines, olives and patches of wheat; groves of sweet chestnuts, walnuts, mulberries and cork-oak, peanuts and pomegranates.

Mediterranean coastlands
In the North is the plain of Catalonia, with its chief town of Barcelona. Behind Valencia, farther to the south, is a broader lowland floored with alluvium brought down by numerous rivers. Farther south again a triangular plain, watered by the river Segura, contains the towns of Alicante, Murcia and Cartagena.

These coastal plains experience almost completely dry summers but wherever water can be obtained from rivers from the mountains, the plains are patterned with channels. Areas that can support two crops each year are known as *huertas* and those with only one crop are *vegas*.

Cultivation is on an intensive garden scale and the main commercial produce are oranges, grapes and almonds; other fruits include figs, peaches, pomegranates, apricots, lemons and even bananas in the South. At Elche, to the south west of Alicante, flourish groves of date palms. And both sugar cane and sugar beet are grown within the same neighbourhood.

Ebro Basin
The Ebro rises in the Cantabrian Mountains only 30 miles from the Bay of Biscay and flows south-eastwards to the Mediterranean. The river breaks through to the coast in a gorge and is building out a delta at its mouth. Its undulating basin, enclosed by uplands and cut off from maritime influences is one of the driest parts of Spain. The green strips of cultivation along the rivers and canals contrast with the dry, brown landscape beyond. Maize, grapes, tobacco, sugar beet, wheat, fruit, vegetables and olives are grown.

Guadalquivar Valley
Drains the lowlands of Andalusia enclosed on the north by the steep edge of the Sierra

Morena, and on the south by the Betic Cordillera. To the south-west of Seville the river breaks into tributaries enclosing marshes, while the coast of the Gulf of Cadiz is bordered with dunes, saltmarsh and lagoons.

The most agriculturally successful area is the valley between Seville and Cordoba where soils are derived from fertile alluvium. The summers are hot and dry and irrigation is necessary. Main products are citrus fruits, including sweet oranges and the bitter 'marmalade' variety grown near Seville, grapes and olives, and even sugar cane and bananas.

PORTUGAL
May be divided into two physical regions.

Margins of the Meseta
The central sierras rise to heights exceeding 200m. The plâteau is crossed by valleys of the Douro, Tagus and Guadiana, as they head towards the Atlantic Ocean.

Portuguese lowlands
Have been grouped as one region but in reality they consist of several subregions with considerable variety. The valley of each westerly flowing river opens out to form a lowland separated by extensions of the Meseta.

Although the coastlands are open to maritime influences from the coast, they lie in a transition zone and the Sierra da Estrella forms a distinct climatic divide. To the north in the Douro plains rainfall is plentiful—no month is rainless.

In the province of Minho, conditions are ideal for cattle-rearing and for the cultivation of maize. Vineyards are widespread on the south-facing slopes of the Douro valley and from the grapes comes the rich wine well known in England as port, so called because it has been shipped from Oporto near the mouth of the Douro since the time of the Crusades.

Further south lie the Coimbra plains and beyond that the lower Tagus valley. Setubal is famous for oranges and Elvas for plums. In the south where the coast turns abruptly eastwards from Cape St Vincent is the coastal plain of Algarve, and due to the rich clay cultivation is on an intensive scale.

Only three ports of any size are found: Oporto in the north, Setubal, the centre of the sardine fisheries and canneries, and Lisbon, the capital city, situated on the banks of the Tagus. Chief exports are cork, wine, sardines, timber and cotton textiles. Manufacturing includes the processing of foodstuffs and the production of paper, glass and pottery.

Corunna harbour

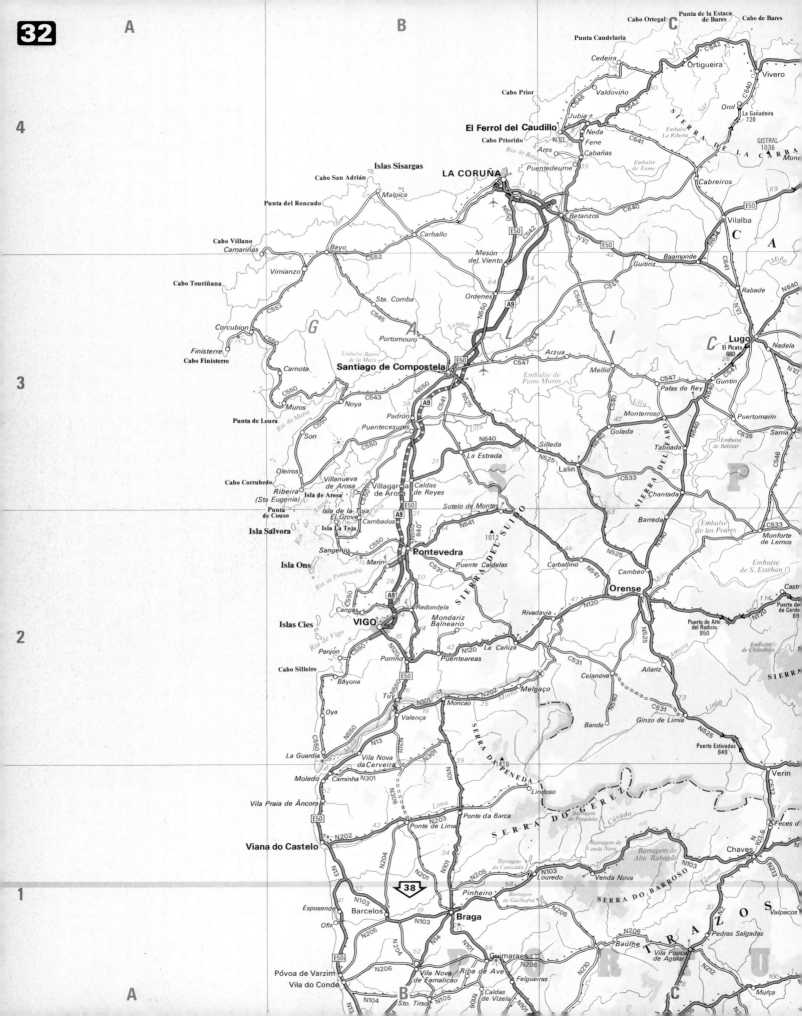

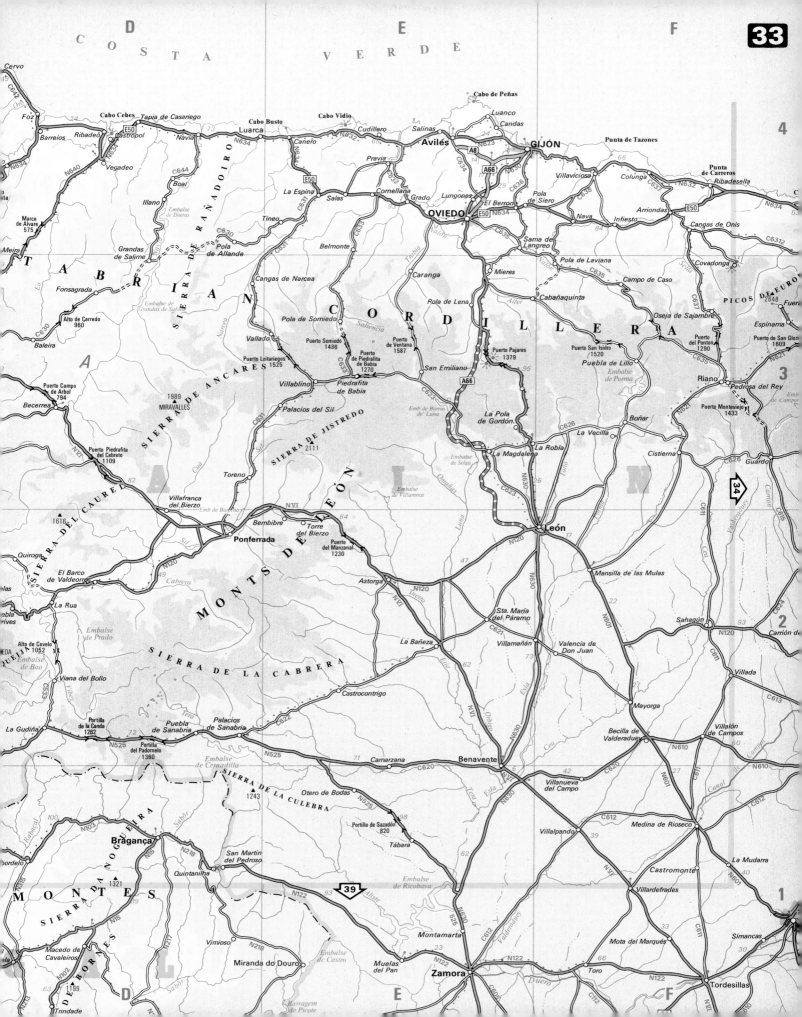

D · E · F

Salses
Port-Barcarès
Estagel
Millas
PERPIGNAN
Canet-Plage
St-Cyprien-Plage
Thuir
Prades
Vernet-les-Bains
Elne
Céret
Amélie-les-Bains
Arles
Le Perthus
La Junquera
Argelès
Le Boulou
Collioure
Port-Vendres
Cap Béar
Banyuls
Cap l'Abeille
Cerbère
Cap Cerbère
Port-Bou
PIC DU CANIGOU
2784
Col d'Ares
1540
Prats-de-Mollo
as de Freser
Camprodón
Llansá
Puerto de la Selva
Cabo Creus
Cadaqués
Figueras
Rosas
Cabo Norfeu
Ampuriabrava
Juan de las Abadesas
Castellfullit de la Roca
Besalú
San Pedro Pescador
Bahia de Rosas
Fluvia
Olot
Collado de Coubet
1010
Vilademat
Bañolas
La Escala
San Quirico de Besora
Estartit
Torroella de Montgri
Embalse de Susqueda
Gerona
La Bisbal
Bagur
Aigua Blava
Palafrugell
Anglés
Embalse de Sau
Llafranch
Calella de Palafrugell
Vich
Sta Coloma de Farnés
Cassá de la Selva
Palamós
San Hilario Sacalm
Playa de Aro
Tona
Llagostera
Sils
Sta Cristina de Aro
S'Agaró
San Feliú de Guixols
Massanet de la Selva
SIERRA DE MONTSENY
1712
Tossa de Mar
Montseny
Tordera
Lloret de Mar
San Celoni
Blanes
Pineda
Calella de la Costa
S. Pol de Mar
Canet de Mar
Arenys de Mar
Caldetas
Granollers
Mataró
Premiá de Mar
Badalona
BARCELONA

COSTA BRAVA

Côte vermeille

MEDITERRANEAN SEA
(MARE MEDITERRANEO)

⊽ **GENOVA**

⊽ **MAHON (MENORCA)**

⊽ **PALMA**

D · E · · F

Kempen

Around each village the sandy soils have gradually been improved by adding humus and fertilisers, and potatoes, wheat, rye, sugar beet and vegetables are grown.

Numerous factories have been built in the heathlands which offered the advantage of cheap land for spacious sites, the accessibility of the port of Antwerp and the proximity of the coalfield. The large scale establishments include zinc, copper and other refineries, chemical works, glass works and stainless steel. Some towns, notably Hasselt and Turnhout, have older established industries: flour mills, distilleries, tobacco factories, brickworks, tanneries etc.

LUXEMBOURG

Consists of two distinct regions. The northern third forms a section of the Ardennes uplands, while the southern is part of the scarplands of Lorraine. The latter is lower, with a milder climate, better soils and more productive agriculture than the Ardennes and so is given the name of the Bon Pays.

Ardennes

Climate is rather bleak and damp, with a well distributed rainfall and snow generally lies for 20-30 days in winter. They do not form a favourable agricultural region, though potatoes and oats are grown as food crops and cattle are kept. Efforts have been made to stimulate livestock breeding and dairying, pastures have been improved by limiting and fertilising, and co-operative dairies collect milk from outlying farms.

Bon Pays

An area of limestone, sandstone and clay ranging in height from 150 to 270m above sea level.

The Moselle Valley in the south-east has a pleasant climate, with long hours of sunshine and about 26in of rainfall. The rest of the Bon Pays is cooler and cloudier than the Moselle Valley.

It is an area of mixed farming; the clays and damp valley floors are under permanent pasture and the lighter sandy and calcareous soils grow cereals, roots and fodder crops. Orchards and vineyards flourish in favoured areas, particularly on south-facing slopes.

The orefield of French Lorraine extends for a few km into Luxembourg, which is fortunate since it has long provided the basis of a flourishing steel industry, and much steel is exported.

Moselle

NETHERLANDS

Sometimes referred to as Holland, though this properly applies only to the two coastal provinces extending northwards from the River Rhine. This is the 'hollow lands' most of which lie below sea level and much of Dutch history has been concerned with the reclamation and defence of their lands.

Coastal lands

From Den Helder to the Hook of Holland —a sweeping curve of sand dunes, strengthened to form a protective barrier for the low-lying lands to the east. Farther north the sand dune line is interrupted forming the West Friesian Islands behind which lies the Wadden Zee, at low tide an area of mud and sand crossed by a maze of dykes, fronts the coast of the mainland.

The area to the south of the Hook of Holland provides the most critical problems of defence against the sea. The 'delta region' with an archipelago of islands separated by channels into which the three rivers pour their waters, requires about 700 miles of dykes.

Delta works

Polders

Behind the sea and river dykes are units of drainage known as polders, about 2,500 in number (some lie below sea level), occupying former areas of the sea or deep lakes, while others would be affected only by high tides or by temporary river flooding. Each polder is surrounded by a dyke and a canal, and pumps raise water for discharge.

Northern coastlands

Comprise much of the provinces of Gröningen and Friesland, forming rich farming country. Nearly all of this area is under rotation grass, clover, potatoes, cereals, chicory and mustard. Friesian cattle graze on the coastal pastures, factory-made butter and cheese is produced and bullocks are raised for beef.

Friesian cattle

Central and southern coastlands

Intensity of agriculture which is rarely equalled. Also presence of large towns with flourishing commerce and industry. Just over half the farmland is under permanent pasture, for the rich peat and clay soils support a thriving dairying activity. In the South milk is consumed in the towns though in the north most is sent to factories for processing into cheese.

Arable farming is most important on the heavy clays of the islands and peninsulas of the delta region. Horticulture and fruit cultivation are carried on in South Holland and to the south of the Hague an extensive area of glasshouses supplies both the towns and a well organised export market. Bulb growing is concentrated on a strip of sandy soil between Leiden and Haarlem east of the dunes and millions of bulbs are exported. The largest city is the capital Amsterdam, situated where the river Amstel enters a bay opening into the SW corner of the former Zuider Zee. A flourishing commercial and financial centre, with a vast range of light and heavy industries.

Rotterdam stands 29km from the sea, to which it is linked by a ship canal, the New Waterway. The port is the biggest in the world, accommodating 6,500 ships annually. Along the New Waterway is the largest industrial district in the Netherlands, the activities include shipyards which can build 500-ton tankers, marine engineering works, Unilever factories making soap and margarine, fine oil refineries, petro-chemical plants, car assembly works, and a range of processing industries. New developments include the construction of Europoort—the world's largest oil terminal.

Rhine—Maas Valley

Forms a distinctive region across the central part of the Netherlands. After the Rhine enters the country it splits up several times into distributaries. The gradients of the rivers are slight and they bring down quantities of clay and sand, gradually raising the level of their beds above the surrounding country.

Heathlands

Three distinct areas separated by broad river valleys. South of the curve of the lower Maas and continuous with the Kempen in Belgium are the heathlands of Noord-Brabant. To the south of the IJssel Meer is the Veluwe, and along the West German frontier are the heathlands of Overjissel, Drenthe and Gröningen.

Parts have been planted with coniferous trees, notably in the Veluwe, and other areas have been sown with drought-resistant grasses. Root crops are grown and cattle are reared, both stall-fed and grazed on permanent pastures, also providing manure for the sandy soils.

South Limburg

A plâteau consisting mainly of chalk in parts covered with sand/clay. A prosperous agricultural district. The loamy soils are excellent for sugar beet and potatoes, there are productive market gardens and orchards and it is important for dairy farming and pig rearing.

The regional centre of South Limburg is Maastricht—an important market centre. It has brick, tile and cement works, a tannery, soap works, several rubber factories, a tobacco-processing factory and one of the largest paper mills in the country.

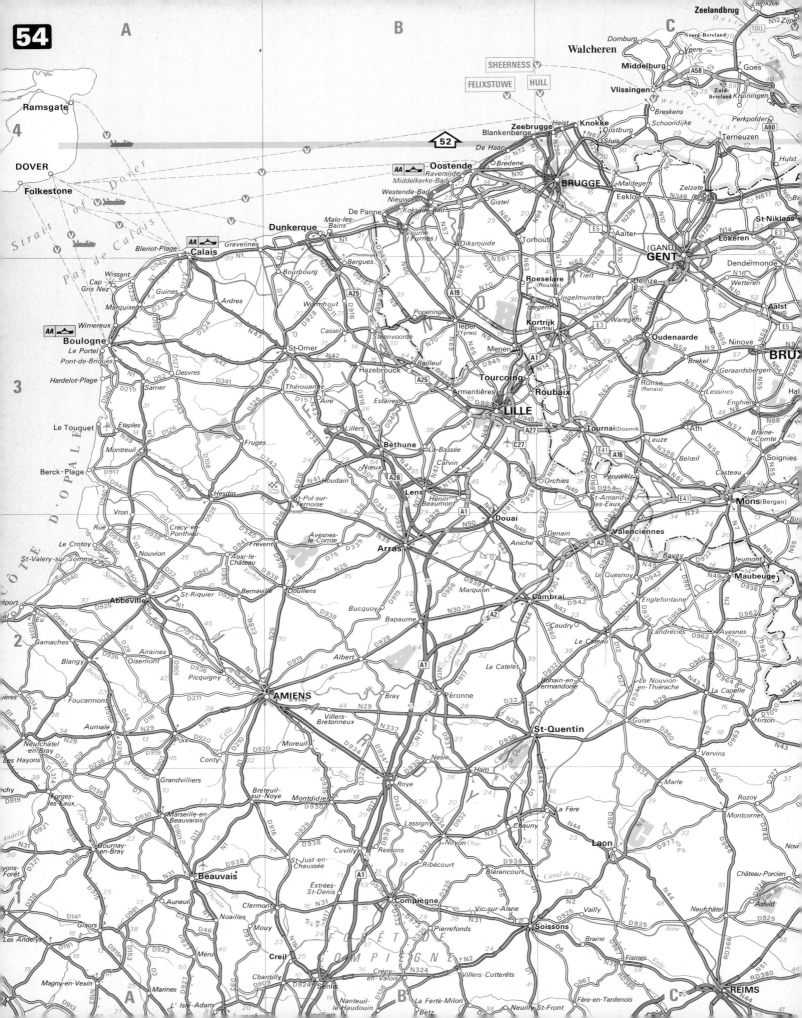

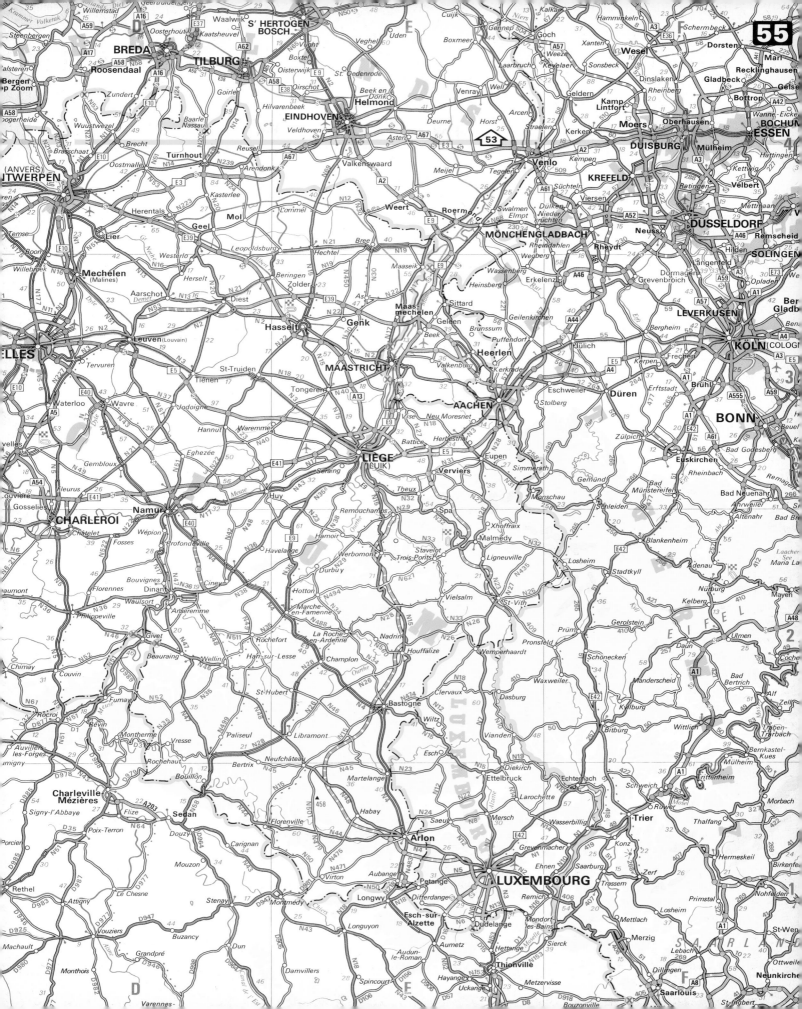

DENMARK

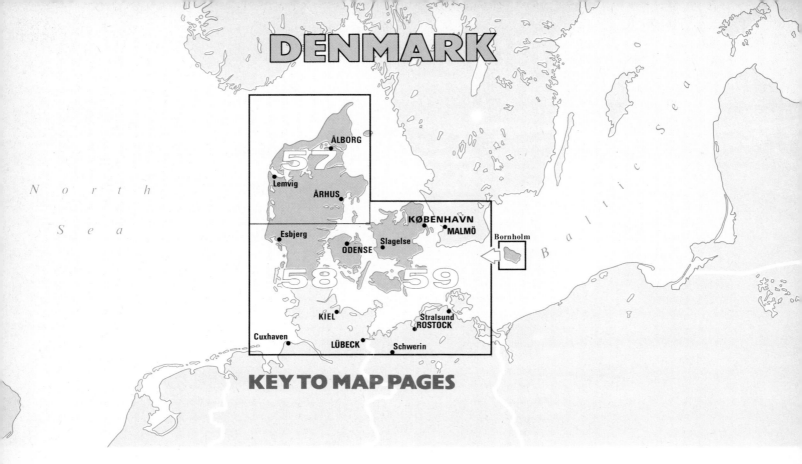

KEY TO MAP PAGES

A glance at the map gives a clue to Denmark's geological history: the mainland of Jutland, the islands in the Kattegat, and Sweden were once joined, and the Baltic was then a lake. With the ending of the Ice Age, sea levels rose till only the tops of the hills were left and the land was cut up by three main channels, the Sound between Zealand and Sweden, Great Belt between Zealand and Funen and Little Belt (now bridged) between Funen and the Jutland mainland.

The great ice sheets had left terminal moraines which form a north-south line of hills in Central Jutland, and pushed sands and gravel to the west of this ridge. These sands form dunes right up the North Sea coast, culminating in a sandy peninsula called the Skaw. To the west of the Skaw is the Skagerrak which divides Denmark and Norway; to the east is the Kattegat which runs between Denmark and Sweden and leads to the Sound and the Baltic Sea.

Much of Eastern Jutland—heath, moorland and bog by nature—has now been reclaimed, and those parts too poor to grow crops have been planted with conifers. Esbjerg in the south east is the main port for trade with Britain. The western part of Jutland and most of the islands have deep fertile soil over chalk and support quite a dense population. With a temperate, moist climate, animal husbandry provides the most efficient use of the land, and concentration on dairying, pig breeding (Denmark claims to be the only country with more pigs than people) and, of recent years, beef production, is economically sound. Only about 10% of the land is permanent pasture, the rest being used in the main for leys and fodder crops.

Mols Hills

Industry is also centred on agriculture, ranging from the manufacture of farm machinery and food processing to glove making. Because Denmark is short of minerals and has no natural fuel supply, industry is centred on sea ports where coal and oil are

unloaded. Power stations consume much of this imported fuel, providing electricity for the home, the farm, food processing and industry generally. The chalk subsoil provides raw material for cement manufacture, while granite for paving and road metal comes from Bornholm, a Danish island in the Baltic. Bornholm also has deposits of kaolin which is the basis of a porcelain industry.

With a fragmented country such as Denmark, communications could be a problem, but difficulties have been efficiently overcome with fine roads and bridges and the provision of inter-island rail ferries. In fact civil engineering know-how is one of Denmark's great assets and Danes act as advisers on projects in many parts of the world. It is appropriate, too, that a nation with a great seafaring tradition should be renowned for shipbuilding and the manufacture of marine engines.

Before the country was intensively and scientifically farmed, much of the eastern part was covered by deciduous forests, which led to a predominance of timber-framed buildings. Clay for brick-making was also available and many of the older buildings use this combination of wood and brick. Places which exemplify this and add historic interest to their visual attractions are the old town of Århus in east Jutland and Odense, home of Hans Christian Andersen, on Funen.

The capital, København (Copenhagen) is situated on the east coast of Zealand, just across the Sound from Sweden, dominating the entrance to the Baltic. It is a fine city, noted particularly for its old merchants' houses and for the Tivoli Gardens.

Unless he goes to the granite isle of Bornholm or the island of Mon, south of Zealand, which has spectacular chalk cliffs, the visitor to Denmark will see flat or gently undulating land, almost all under cultivation.

Skagen

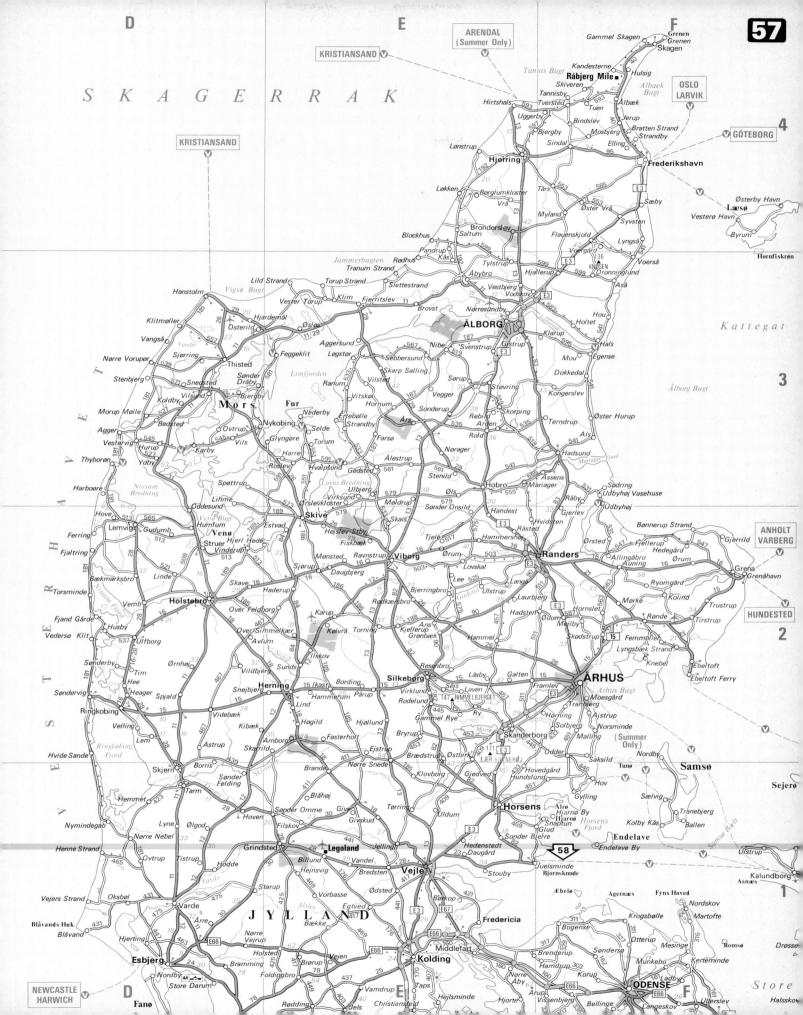

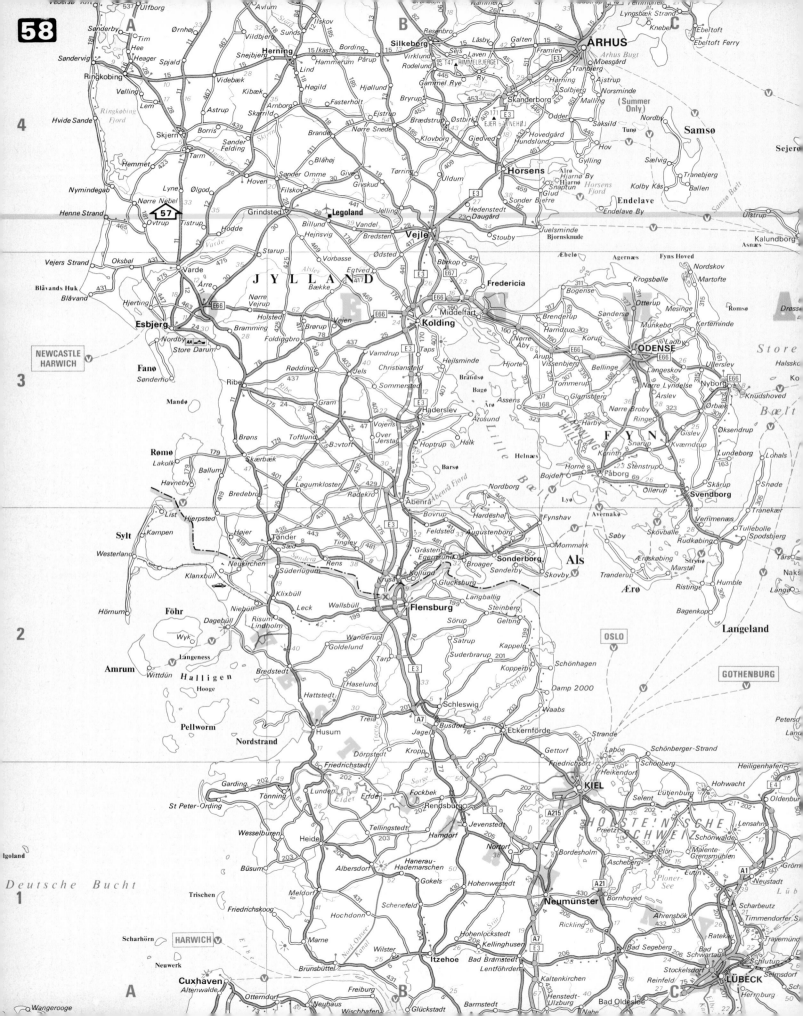

GERMANY

North Sea

Baltic Sea

KIEL
Cuxhaven
LÜBECK
HAMBURG
BREMERHAVEN
GRONINGEN
BREMEN

Stralsund
ROSTOCK
Schwerin
Neubrandenburg
SZCZECIN
Salzwedel
Gorzów Wielkopolski

62 · 63 · 64 · 65

Zwolle
HANNOVER
ENSCHEDE
BIELEFELD
ARNHEM
ESSEN
DÜSSELDORF
KASSEL

BERLIN
MAGDEBURG
Zielona Góra
Cottbus
LEIPZIG
DRESDEN

66 · 67 · 68 · 69

KÖLN
BONN
SIEGEN
Koblenz
FRANKFURT-AM-MAIN
LUXEMBOURG
MANNHEIM

ERFURT
KARL-MARX-STADT
PRAHA
Bayreuth
PLZEN
NÜRNBERG

70 · 71 · 72 · 73

METZ
NANCY
STUTTGART
STRASBOURG
Ulm
Épinal
Kempten
BASEL
ZÜRICH

REGENSBURG
České Budějovice
Landshut
Passau
LINZ
MÜNCHEN
SALZBURG

74 · 75 · 76 · 77

KEY TO MAP PAGES

Germany not only lies at the geographic crossroads of Europe, it lies also at the subcontinent's economic and political heart. West Germany (GFR) holds not only much of the economic future of Western Europe in her hands, but also much of the political future of Eastern Europe as well.

Northern Plains

Glaciated by the Continental ice sheets moving out of Scandinavia. These areas comprise some of the most sterile soils in all of Germany. For the most part clothed only in heather and pines. One of the most extensive of such areas is the Luneburg Heath, just south of Hamburg.

In sharp contrast to these unproductive heathlands are the loess soils that form an almost continuous belt across the front of the Central Uplands. They represent the accummulation of fine, wind-blown dust whisked off the ice front by glacial winds and deposited where the force of the wind was broken by the obstacle posed by the Central Uplands.

These soils are among the most fertile in

Germany and early on gave rise to a dense agricultural settlement. Indeed, many of the leading towns of medieval Germany grew up as market centres for the rich agricultural hinterlands of the loess belt, including Munster, Hanover, Braunschweig, Magdeburg, Leipzig and Dresden.

Through most of the northern plain, hay, rye, and potatoes constitute the chief crops, with wheat, sugar beets and vegetables being grown on the better loess soils. Mixed farming is the general rule, and milk and meat are the major sources of income for most farmers. In many of the sandy heathlands a sustained yield production of conifers is helping to meet Germany's needs for construction timber and wood pulp and along the north-west coast commercial fishing contributes to the local economy as well.

Apart from a small oil field in the Holstein District north of Hamburg, most of the commercial mineral deposits of the northern plain lie along its southern margin.

Along the edge of the Central Uplands in the

Terraced landscape

60

East German sector there are large deposits of lignite or brown coal, salt and potash, as well as smaller deposits of bituminous coal.

Although the latter are inadequate for Germany's industrial needs, coal is imported from Poland and iron ore is supplied by the Soviet Union. East Germany (GDR) emerges as one of the major industrial powers of the Communist orbit. Indeed, its exports of steel, heavy chemicals, machinery, motor vehicles, machine tools, optical goods and textiles to East European trading partners give it a healthy balance of payments.

In the West German sector, there are salt, potash and oil deposits in the Braunschweig-Hanover area, and the former city has a variety of food processing, chemical and engineering industries.

The largest industrial concentration in West Germany is located in the valley of the Ruhr River. Owes its industrial pre-eminence to a combination of factors, primarily to its location on the largest deposit of high-grade coal in Europe, but also to its location adjacent to one of the great navigable rivers of the subcontinent. Through the Rhine and its interconnecting system of canals, as well as by means of a highly developed railway network, the Ruhr has managed to supply large areas of Western Europe with coal, while at the same time giving rise to an agglomeration of industries that makes it the economic nerve centre of West Germany.

Saar and Saarburg

Heavy metallurgy, chemicals and engineering are the principal industrial emphasis of the Ruhr, but all manner of lighter manufacturing is represented as well.

Central Uplands

A jumbled landscape of low forested ridges, most of them scarcely reaching 3,000ft elevation, and open, cultivated valleys. Broadleaf deciduous trees predominate, but conifers are also found at higher elevations and where reforestation projects are under way. The region's geology is diverse, with older crystalline rocks forming many of the ridges in the west and accounting in part for the narrow and scenic Rhine gorge, some sedimentaries and volcanic areas. The soils of the valleys and basins are more fertile than those of the Plain and much of the land is in pasture and a mixed livestock crop economy prevails. Among the cereals, wheat, barley, rye and oats are all represented, and there is likewise a consider-

Oberweser

able production of potatoes, vegetables, sugar beets, oil seeds, hops and fruit.

Most of the forests of the Central Uplands are carefully managed and a variety of wood-using industries are scattered throughout the region. However, apart from iron ore deposits in the Sieg River valley, the Central Uplands have only minor deposits of copper and lead. Thus, with no mineral wealth to speak of and few valleys or basins large or productive enough to generate major commercial centres, the Central Uplands can be characterised as an area of small to medium sized towns and cities.

Rhine Graben

Was formed by the buckling of a large segment of the earth's crust, followed by the downfaulting of its centre. One side of the fault is represented by the Vosges mountains of France; the other side is composed of the Schwarzwald (Black Forest).

Because the valley lies below 500ft elevation and the rain shadow of the Vosges, it constitutes the warmest and driest region in Germany. Thus, in terms of terrain, soils and climate, the Rhine Graben represents the country's premier agricultural region, an area whose crops include grapes, tobacco and corn, as well as wheat, sugar beets, stone fruits, hops and vegetables.

Alpine Foreland

Has been glaciated and has infertile morainic soils. Its rolling surface varies from less than 700ft to over 2,200ft in elevation, so despite its location in the far south, its summer temperatures are cool and its winters are cold and snowy.

Located at the foot of the Alps, it is a favourite area of tourists in both summer and winter. But agriculture is chiefly based on hay and dairying, and the most important field crops are potatoes, oats and barley.

Large areas of the poorer sandy soils are in conifers, as are the lower slopes of the mountains, so forestry is locally important. The prevalence of soft woods is likewise reflected in the greater frequency of wooden houses than in central and northern Germany.

Black Forest

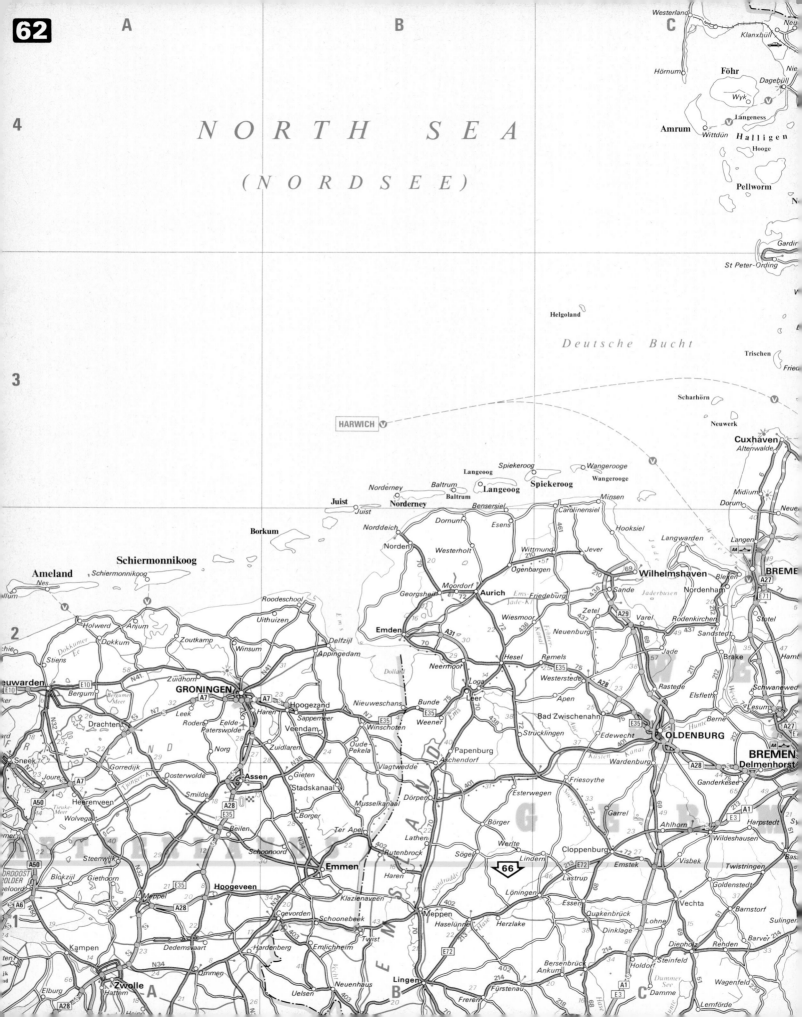

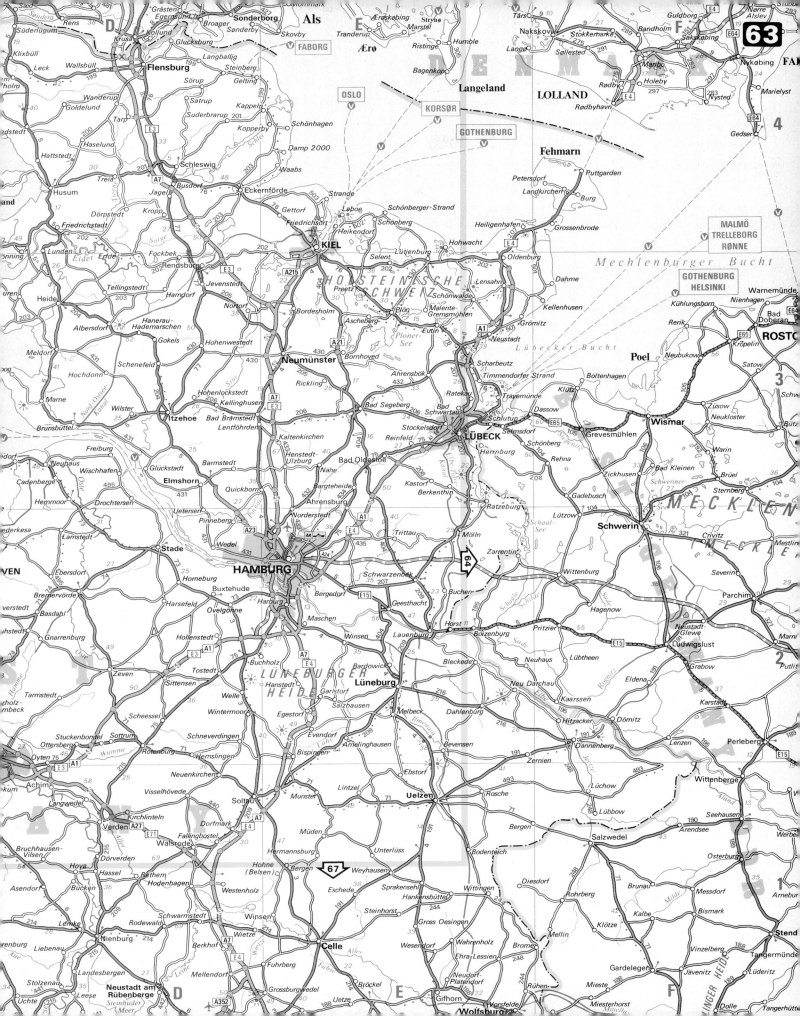

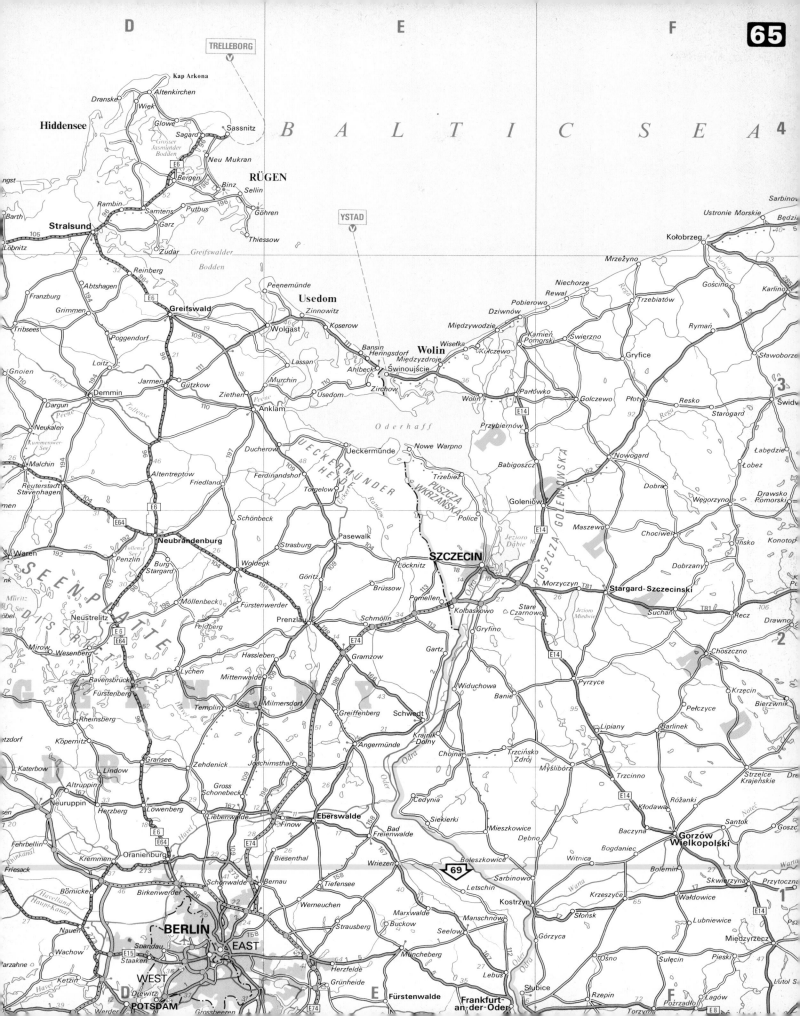

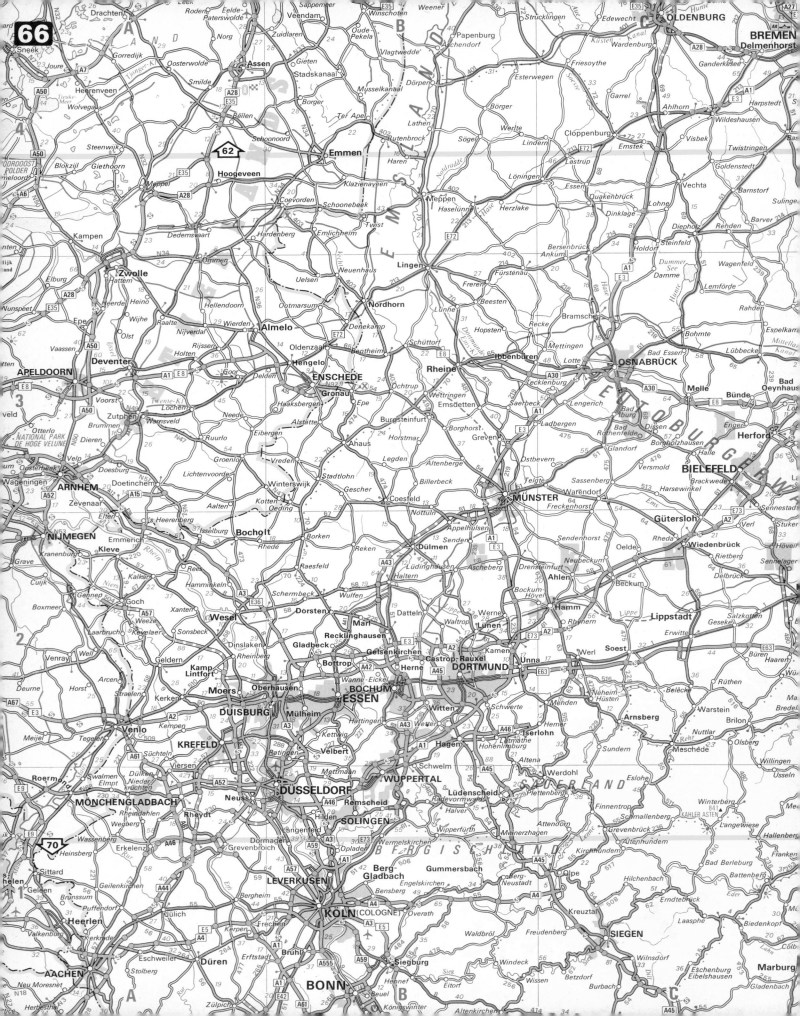

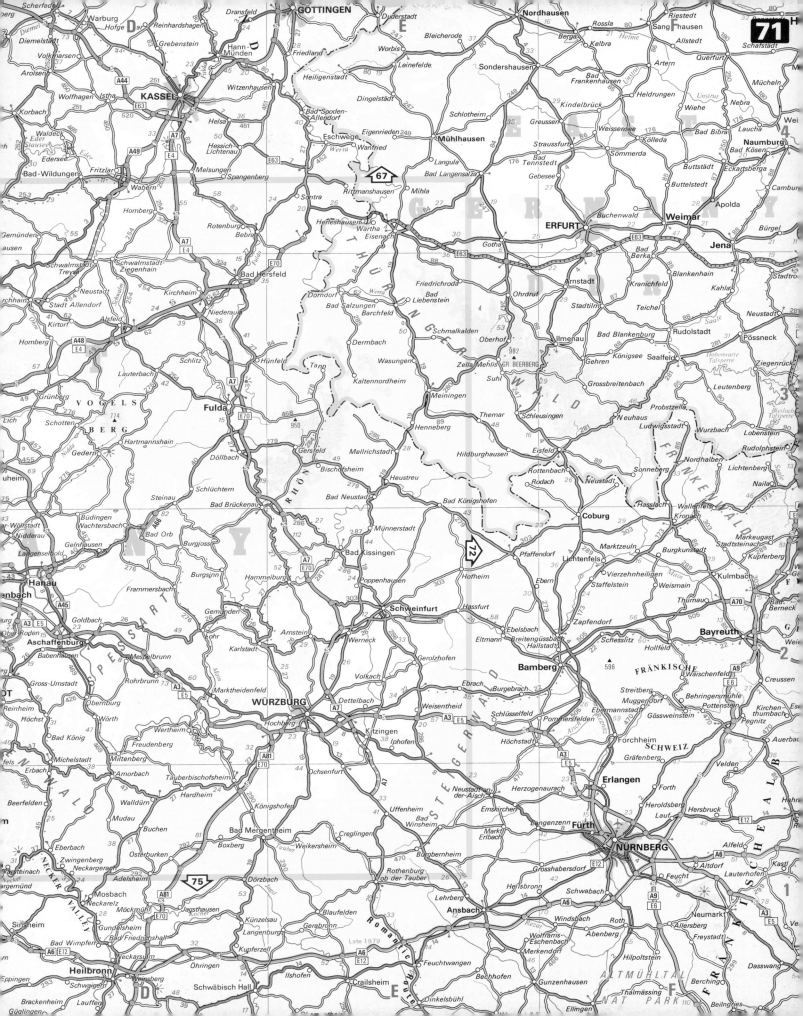

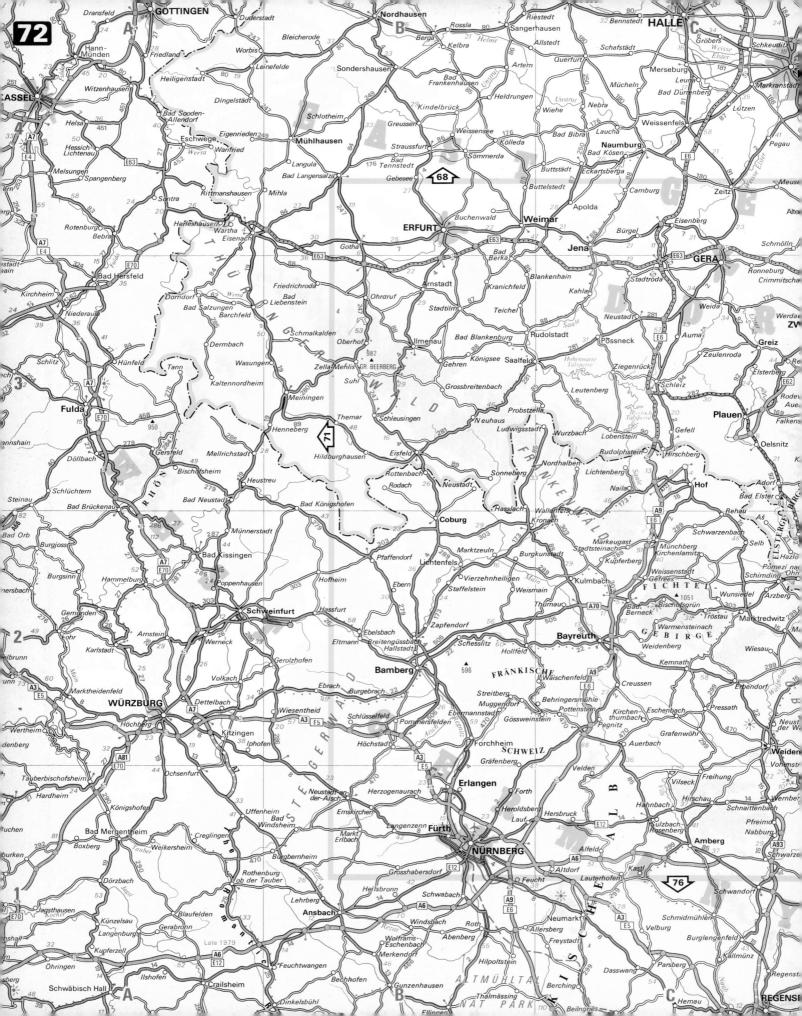

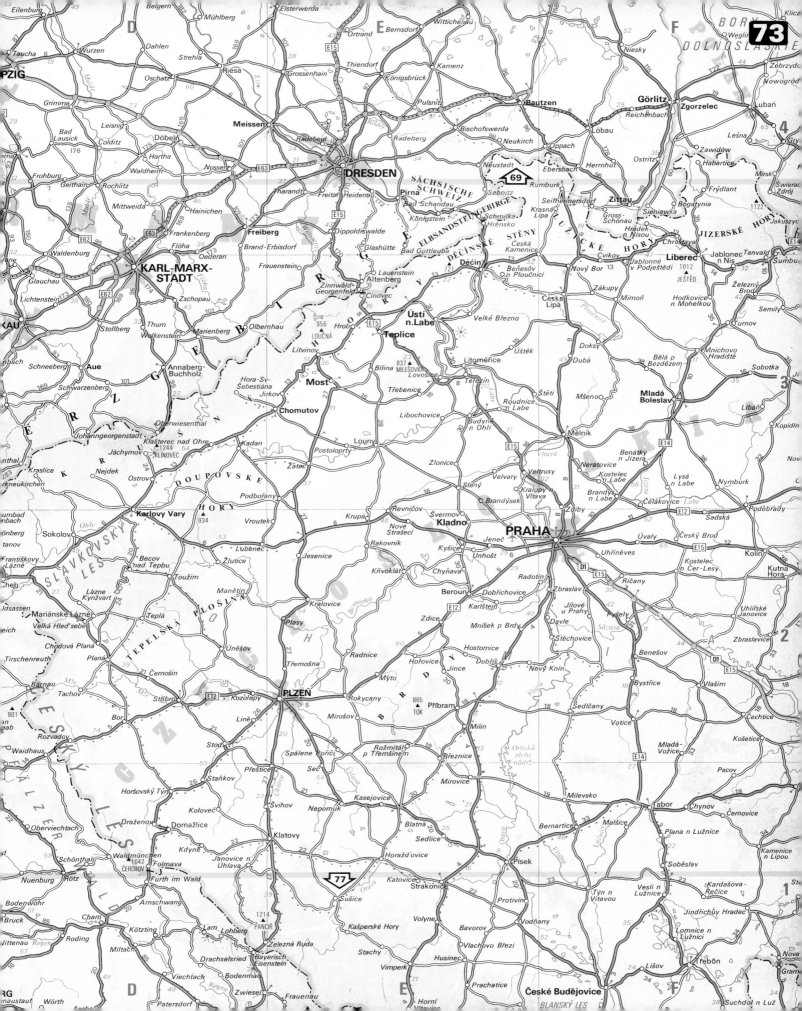

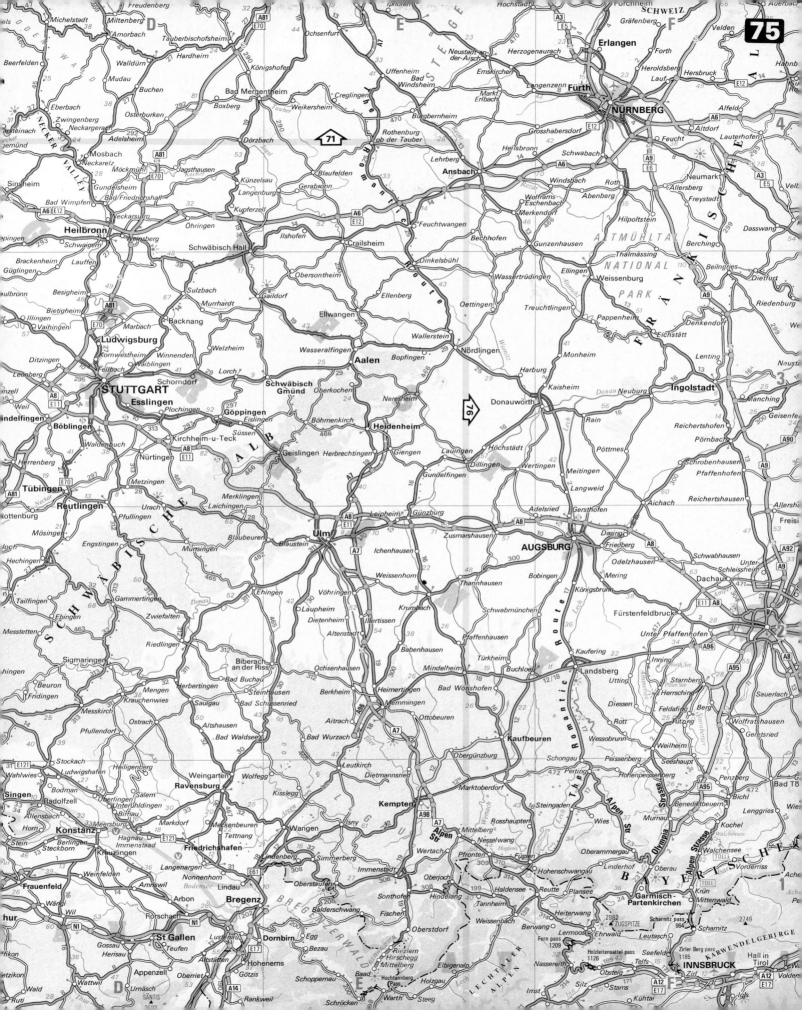

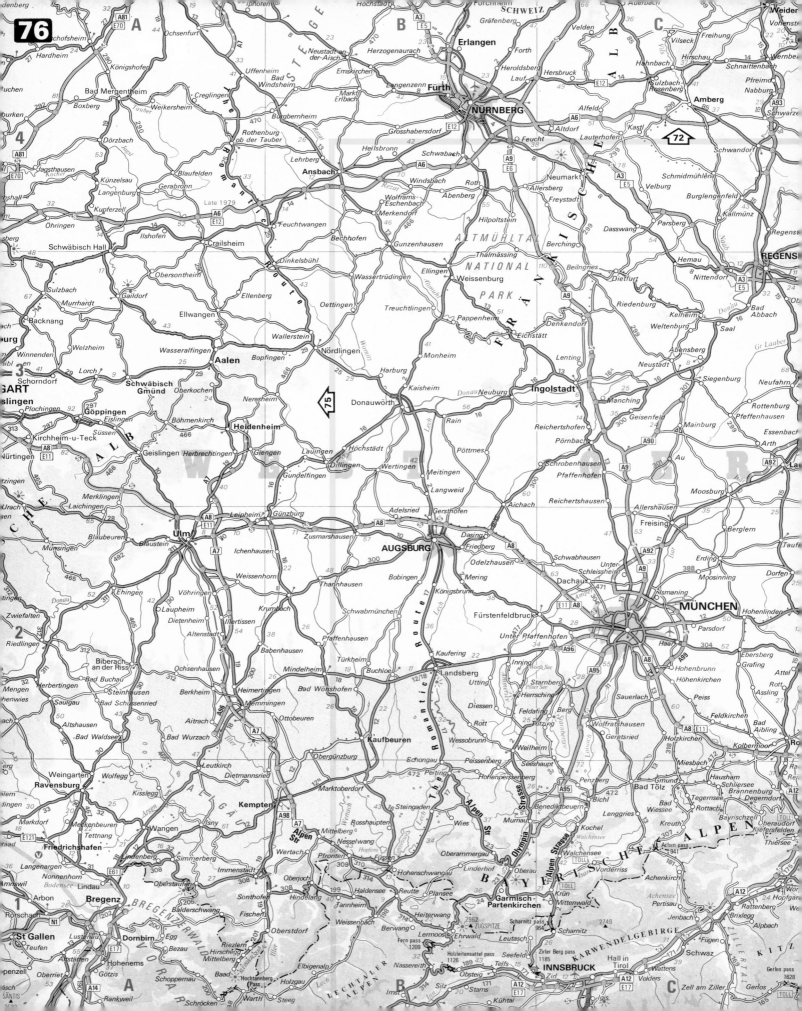

SWITZERLAND & AUSTRIA

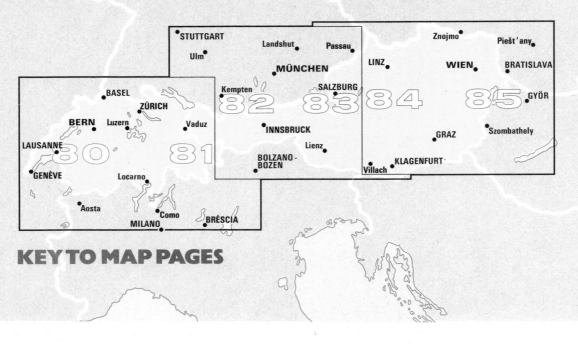

STUTTGART
Ulm
Landshut
Passau
Znojmo
Pieš´t´any
MÜNCHEN
LINZ
WIEN
BRATISLAVA
BASEL
Kempten
SALZBURG
82
83 **84**
85
GYÖR
ZÜRICH
BERN
Luzern
Vaduz
INNSBRUCK
Lienz
GRAZ
Szombathely
LAUSANNE
30
81
BOLZANO-
BOZEN
KLAGENFURT
GENÈVE
Locarno
Villach
Aosta
Como
BRÉSCIA
MILANO

KEY TO MAP PAGES

As one travels eastwards from Switzerland into the Ötzthal Alps of Austria, little difference is appreciable in the landscape and the people. Thickly forested slopes rise from green-carpeted valleys to peaks and snowfields. The chalet villages are strikingly similar and both nationalities carry on cattle-rearing, forestry and catering for tourists.

And yet, of course, there *are* differences. Austria is twice as large and has more mineral wealth including iron ore, salt, graphite, lead, zinc and oil. Nevertheless despite a lack of raw materials Switzerland has for so long been the more prosperous, with important industrial activities in Zürich, Basle, Bern and Geneva.

Silver thistle

SWITZERLAND

Has been able to maintain her neutrality for centuries, and at the same time has benefited from her central position in Europe. She consists of a federation of 25 cantons which maintain a considerable degree of political independence and there is a strong local feeling, emphasised by the isolation of many parts and by differences in religion and language. Of the total population, 70% speak German, mainly in the centre and north. In the western cantons French is generally spoken, in Ticino in the extreme south Italian is used and in the south-easterly canton of Graubünden nearly 60,000 speak *Romansch,* a language which has developed from Latin; all four are officially recognised.

Swiss Alps

In the north is the Bernese Oberland with crystalline peaks such as the Jungfrau and the Eiger with their rock ridges and ice-covered faces rising abruptly from these snowfields, the largest being the Aletsch, while from the Rhone Glacier the river takes its source emerging through an ice cave.

Eiger, Mönch and Jungfrau

To the south a narrow trench runs parallel to the ranges from the NE and SW. Its western section is occupied by the Rhone and this part is known as Valais.

The Rhine flows in the opposite direction along the eastern section as far as Chur where it bends northwards towards Lake Constance.

To the south of the Rhone-Rhine trough are the main Alpine ranges—which follow to a large extent the Swiss-Italian frontier.

The mountains known in the west as the Pennine Alps, are higher than in the Bernese Oberland, rising to such fine summits as Monte Rosa and the pyramid peak of the Matterhorn. Farther east the mountains are lower but still impressive, separated by such deeply cut valleys as that of the Inn.

There are about 700 square miles of glaciers and permanent snowfields. In the Ice Age, they were, of course, more extensive, and they have left their mark in the form of deeply eroded valleys, often containing lakes, and at their lower ends and on the lands beyond are moraines and deposits of clay.

Even in the high valleys some agriculture is carried on. Cereals, root crops and hay are grown on the valley sides, orchards and vines are sited on the south-facing slopes, cheese is produced and wood is used for fuel, chalet building and wood-carving.

Wood-carving

Also, industry is prevalent, for the Alps provide a vast source of power and hydro-electric schemes, utilising high-level reservoirs, have been established.

Swiss Jura
The Jura mountains form an arc which extends across the Franco–Swiss frontier. Parallel folded sedimentary ranges, culminating in limestone clefts with craggy crests are separated by steep-sided valleys. In the lower valleys, rivers break through, forming gorges.

Generally the Jura are thickly forested with conifers that are carefully maintained. Regular replanting follows felling. The valley floors are covered with rich meadowland on which are kept cattle supplying factories making condensed milk, chocolate and Gruyere cheese.

Cheese-making

Prosperous cottage industries such as carving and the manufacture of clocks and watches thrive.

Swiss Plateau
An undulating area of sandstone covered in most places with clays and sands laid down during the Ice Age. However, the surface is far from flat, wooded ridges rise above the general level, lakes lie in hollows and the Aar and Reuss flow northwards in steep-sided valleys to the Rhine.

In some parts the marshy floors of former lakes have been drained as between Lakes Bienne and Neuchâtel. About two thirds of the Swiss population live in this region, for here are both intensive agriculture and large industrial towns.

More than half the farmland is under pasture and fodder crops, sugar beet, potatoes and cereals are grown. Orchards grow apples, pears and black cherries; much fruit is used for yogurt and jam-making.

Considerable developments have taken place in the production of hydro-electricity; the large Mooserboden dam and reservoir in the Hohe-Tauern were completed as part of a major project in the Kaprum valley.

AUSTRIA
Austria has a population of 7.4 million—approximately a third live in five cities, while by contrast another third live in small towns and villages among the valleys and basins separated by mountains. Nearly two-fifths is covered with forest which provides raw material. In spite of the extent of mountains, farming is important, for arable land occupies a fifth of the area, post-War improvements enable the country to supply three-quarters of its food needs.

In addition to a diversified agriculture, Austria has timber, water power and all the basic ingredients of heavy industry, iron ore, coal, petroleum and natural gas.

The country may be divided into five regions of which three are predominantly mountainous.

Vorarlberg and Tirol Oberdrum
Occupy the most westerly part of the country. Long, narrow region of mountains interspersed by high valleys. Voralberg slopes westwards to the Rhine valley and Lake Constance while the Tirol consists of a deep valley of the Inn, flanked on the north by the limestone peaks of the Bavarian Alps and on the south by the ridges of the Ötzthal and Zillerthal Alps.

These are dotted with small snowfields and glaciers and the snow hump of the Wildspitzen.

Agricultural activities include dairy farming, the cultivation of maize, barley and root crops, fruit-growing on the sunnier slopes and forestry on the hillsides.

Oberdrum

Southern mountains and valley
The southern part of this region consists of the broad valley of the Drava which flows eastwards to join the Danube in Yugoslavia. This valley is bordered by the frontier ridges of the Carnic and Karawanken Alps, and fertile basins with some attractive lakes. Agriculture flourishes. Vineyards and orchards are to be found among the meadows while pine forests are grown. Styria is often referred to as 'the green province'.

Tourists are well catered for and varied industries include making paper, wooden articles, textiles, embroidery and small metal goods.

Northern mountains and valleys
The Bavarian Alps continue eastward from near Salzburg, splaying out and becoming lower as they approach the Danube and forming a landscape of limestone crags, forested ridges, gorges and lakes.

Alpine foreland/Danube Valley
In the province of Upper Austria between the Alpine ranges and the Danube, lies the easterly portion of the Alpine foreland. Wooded sandstone ridges, rich valley pastures and lakes make this a pleasant countryside. The land slopes northwards to the Danube which enters Austria below Passau and flows eastwards to Vienna.

Between the Danube and the Czechoslovakian frontier the ancient rocks of the Bohemian Plâteau extend into Austria. This is forested, but the valleys have been cleared for cultivation.

Vienna Basin
The heart of Austria, and consists of a lowland between the easterly spurs of the Alps and the foothills of the Carpathians. Not only important agriculturally, but also because it contains both oil and gas fields. Although production has levelled off—these deposits have allowed the Austrians to establish major refineries and petrochemical factories in the area. In a sense, they can also be said to round out Austria's resource picture, for in sum the country will be seen to have one of the most balanced economic endowments of any nation in Europe.

Aerial view of Vienna

This basin is covered with vineyards: the Wienerwald (the renowned 'Vienna Woods' of Johann Strauss) is a resort for the Viennese and its produce includes many pleasant white wines.

ITALY

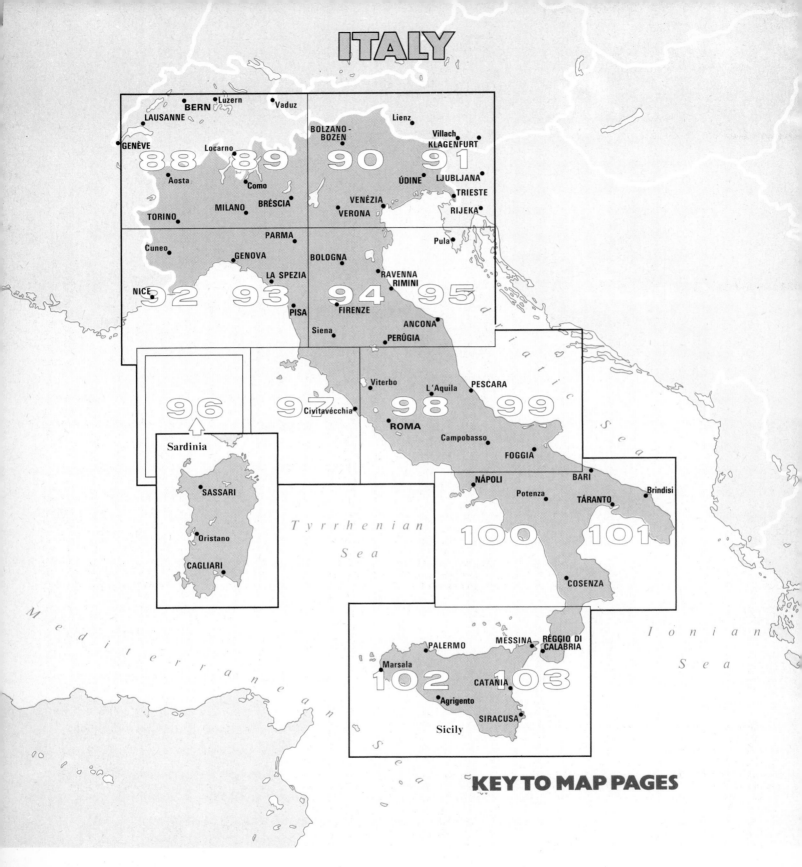

Bern · Luzern · Vaduz
LAUSANNE
GENÈVE
88 89
Aosta · Locarno · Como
TORINO · MILANO · BRÉSCIA

Lienz
BOLZANO-BOZEN · Villach
90 91 · KLAGENFURT
ÚDINE · LJUBLJANA
VENÉZIA · TRIESTE
Verona · RIJEKA

PARMA
Cuneo · GENOVA · BOLOGNA · Pula
LA SPEZIA · RAVENNA
92 93 94 95 · RIMINI
NICE · PISA · FIRENZE · ANCONA
Siena · PERÚGIA

Viterbo · L'Aquila · PESCARA
96 97 98 99
Sardinia · Civitavécchia · ROMA
SASSARI · Campobasso
· FOGGIA

Oristano
CAGLIARI · NÁPOLI · BARI
Potenza · Brindisi
100 101 · TÁRANTO

Tyrrhenian Sea

COSENZA

PALERMO · MESSINA · RÉGGIO DI CALABRIA
Marsala
102 103
CATANIA
Agrigento · SIRACUSA
Sicily

Mediterranean · *Ionian Sea*

KEY TO MAP PAGES

Consists of a peninsula with a mountainous 'backbone' projecting southwards into the Mediterranean, together with the basin of the River Po (North Italian Plain) bordered on the north by the Alps, and a number of islands. Marked contrasts exist between northern Italy on the one hand and the peninsula and islands on the other, both of climate and land use.

In the Alpine region the climate varies

according to altitude and aspect; parts near the lakes experience mild winters, though the mountains are snow-covered. In the northern plain the climate is one of extremes, with distinctly cold winters and warm summers and with a well distributed rainfall.

In peninsular Italy Mediterranean influences are dominant, though the mountains have cold winters with a good deal of snow.

Farther south winters are milder and summers hot and sunny with high midday temperatures.

The Italian mainland can be divided into five distinct regions with, in addition, the islands of Sicily and Sardinia.

Alpine Ranges
They curve round the western and northern margins of the North Italian Plain and the

Aquila

frontiers with France, Switzerland and Austria.

Apart from these ridges, Italy also has the Bergamo Alps in the centre and the Dolomites in the east, which can boast magnificent pinnacles rising steeply above the pinewoods and meadows of the lower slopes and valley floors.

The Dolomites

Villages and farms are situated in the valleys and hay and cereals are grown. Cattle and sheep are pastured on the hills and the slopes have sheltered orchards which enable such fruits as peaches, apricots, grapes and olives to be grown. Much of the mountains are forested, which creates much lumber and timber work.

North Italian Plain
Extends for about 250m from the Alpine foothills in the west to the Adriatic Sea.

The Plain is covered with alluvium, finer silt in the centre along the line of the main river and coarser sands and gravel nearer the margins. To the north much material is glacial in origin, deposited when glaciers extended farther south.

As far as agriculture is concerned, the Plain can be divided into a central zone along the river, including the Po delta, a middle irrigated zone and drier marginal zones flanking the Alpine and Appenine foothills.

The central zone is the most fertile, obtaining water from the Po delta. The land is flat with lines of poplars and fruit trees. Such crops as maize, wheat, fodder crops and rice are grown. Stall-fed cattle are kept, the milk being used to produce Parmesan and Gorgonzola cheeses.

Vista of Belluno

Appenines
Consist of mountain ranges which extend for about 600m. In the North, the mountains bordering the coast are known as the Ligurian Appenines, and are dissected by valleys and in places are forested with sweet chestnut. The rocks are varied, consisting of sandstone, limestone and clay, or marble, as at Carrara.

The Southern Appenines were more a series of isolated blocks rather than a continuous chain. They are rugged and in the west volcanic activity is evident.

West Coast
Small areas of lowland separated by spurs, ending in rocky peninsulas. This is the Italian Riviera with its many international resorts—San Remo, Alassio—which provides wines, olives, citrus fruits and flowers.

The next lowland area is the basin of the Arno which drains central Tuscany. It is a fertile district growing hard wheat (for macaroni), olives and vines; the last flourish on the slopes of the neighbouring Chianti; hills which have given their name to Italy's most famous wine.

The coastal plain opens out again where it is crossed by the Tiber, with Rome situated on its banks.

The only other west coast lowlands of any size are the Plain of Naples and the area bordering the Gulf of Salerno. Very fertile soil enables vineyards and orchards. Figs and tomatoes are both plentiful. The chief town is Naples, an important industrial centre with oil refineries, cotton mills and canning factories.

Bay of Naples

East Coast Plain
The Adriatic coast is straight with few indentations and, due to the help of irrigation, is generally well cultivated. The whole area is fairly densely populated, many of the local population being employed in Ancona, Bari and Brindisi.

SICILY
The Island of Sicily is separated by the Strait of Messina from mainland Italy. The northern edge of the island is bordered by rugged limestone hills—the Sicilian Appenines.

The rainy season is almost entirely confined to the autumn and winter months. The high temperatures of summer cause rapid evaporation and so emphasise the drought. Yet despite this, Sicily does have a profitable agriculture. Soils are fertile, especially around the flanks of Mt Etna, where almonds and peaches are produced. Vegetables, especially tomatoes, are grown intensively. On the lower slopes are many lemon groves; Sicily is still the chief exporter of this fruit. Higher up, the Sicilians grow oranges, tangerines, citrons and almonds. The vine is grown both for wine and for table grapes. A few varieties such as Marsala are exported.

Much of the interior undulating sandstone plâteau consists of extensive farmlands growing wheat and beans in rotation during the winter. Sheep and goats are grazed on the upland pastures, sulphur is mined near Caltanisetta and limestone is quarried for making cement.

SARDINIA
In spite of improvements in economic expansion, manufacturing and tourism since the end of the Second World War, Sardinia remains thinly populated and not very productive. Winter wheat is grown but with low yields, and vines and olives are cultivated on terraced slopes. Some minerals are worked, notably lead and zinc, and a little iron ore and coal.

Least typically Mediterranean in its physical character, much of the island is eroded, crystalline granite strewn with boulders and dotted by clumps of prickly pear.

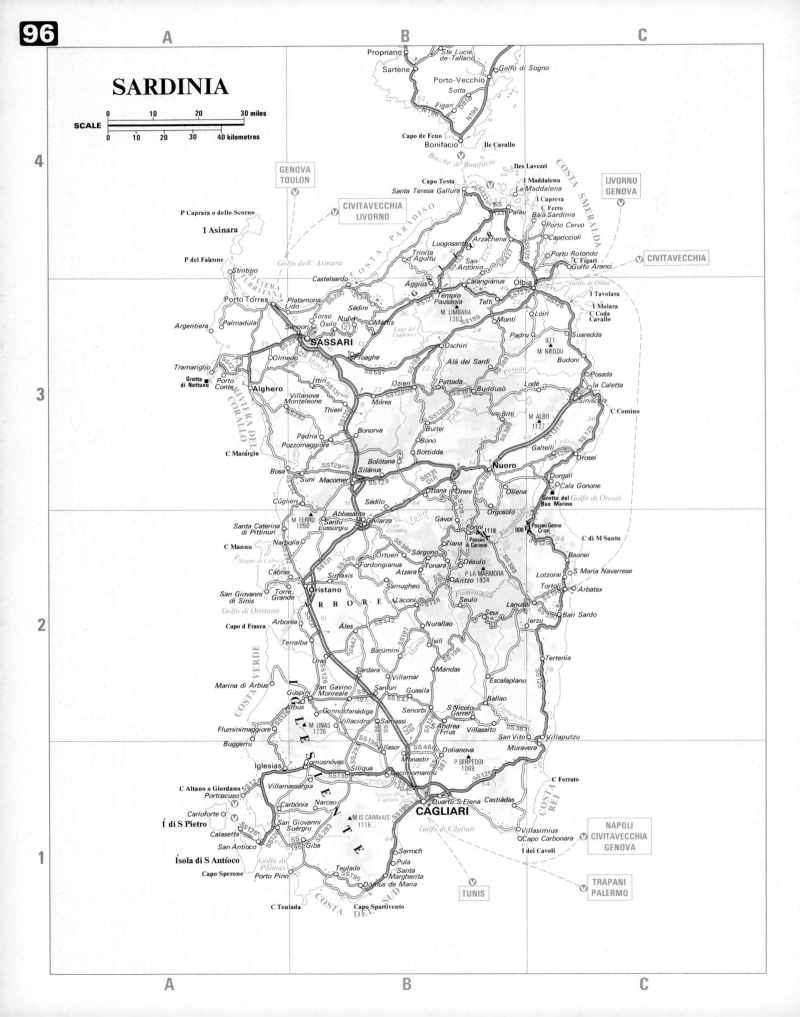

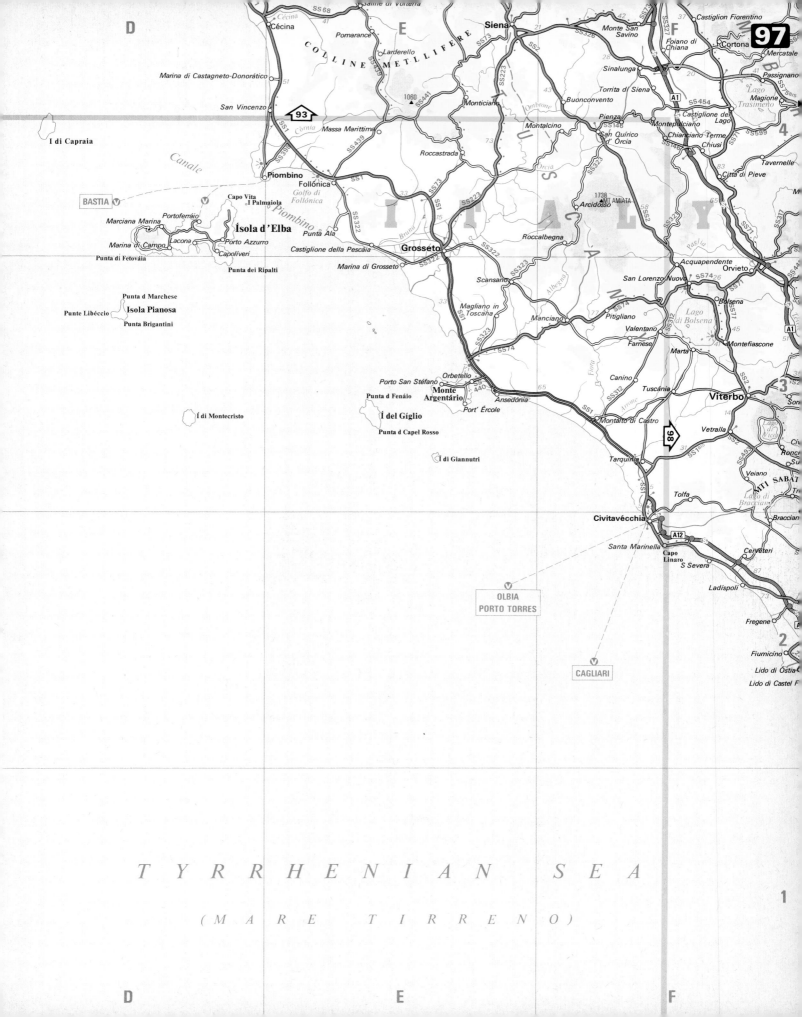

D

E

F

Cécina
SS68
Saline di Volterra

COLLINE METALLIFERE

Siena

Pomarance

Larderello

SS441

Monticiano

SS2

Monte San Savino

Castiglion Fiorentino

Foiano di Chiana

Cortona

Mercatale

A1

Passignano

Lago Trasimeno

Magione

Marina di Castagneto-Donorático

1060

Massa Marittima

SS439

Roccastrada

SS73

SS223

Buonconvento

Pienza

Sinalunga

Torrita di Siena

SS326

Montepulciano

Castiglione del Lago

Chianciano Terme

SS599

SS146

Montalcino

San Quírico d' Órcia

Chiusi

Tavernelle

Città di Pieve

93

SS1

San Vincenzo

Córnia

I di Capraia

Canale

BASTIA

Capo Vita

I Palmaiola

Portoferráio

Marciana Marina

Ísola d'Elba

Porto Azzurro

Punta Ala

Golfo di Follónica

Follónica

Piombino

SS398

Piombino

SS322

SS322

Castiglione della Pescáia

SS1

SS223

Brana

Órcia

Ombrone

Arcidosso

1738 MT AMIATA

Roccalbegna

SS2

Paglia

SS71

Acquapendente

Orvieto

A1

Marina di Campo

Lacona

Capolíveri

Punta di Fetováia

Punta dei Ripalti

Marina di Grosseto

Grosseto

SS322

SS323

Scansano

SS74

San Lorenzo Nuovo

SS74

Bolsena

SS71

Punta d Marchese

Isola Pianosa

Punte Libéccio

Punta Brigantini

Magliano in Toscana

SS323

Albenia

Manciano

SS74

Pitigliano

Valentano

Farnese

Lago di Bolsena

Montefiascone

SS2

A1

Í di Montecristo

SS574

Fiora

Canino

Marta

Tuscánia

SS312

SS2

Porto San Stéfano

Orbetello

Monte Argentário

Ansedónia

SS440

SS1

65

Arrone

Montalto di Castro

Viterbo

SS675

Punta d Fenáio

Í del Gíglio

Port' Ércole

98

Vetralla

SS1

SS675

Veiano

MTI SABAT

Punta d Capel Rosso

Tarquínia

Í di Giannutri

Tolfa

Lago di Bracciano

Bracciano

Civitavécchia

A12

Santa Marinella

Capo Linaro

S Severa

Cervéteri

Ladíspoli

OLBIA
PORTO TORRES

Fregene

2

CAGLIARI

Fiumicino

Lido di Óstia

Lido di Castel F

4

3

2

TYRRHENIAN SEA

(MARE TIRRENO)

1

4

TYRRHENIAN SEA

(MARE TIRRENO)

I Alicudi

GENOVA

NAPOLI

CAGLIARI
TUNIS

GENOVA

Isola delle
Fémmine   Capo Gallo

P Ráisi   Mondello

Capo S Vito

San Vito lo Capo

Cínisi   Capaci

SS 113

AA   C Zafferano

PALERMO

CAGLIARI

I
Maréttimo

I di Lévanzo

ISOLE ÉGADI

I Favignana

Trápani   Erice   SS 187

Castellammare
del Golfo

Golfo di Castellammare

A29

Monreale   SS 186

Bagheria

SS 113   Golfo di Términi Immerse

Cefalù   San Ste
di Cama

3

Paceco   SS 113

DIR
A29

Calatafimi

Alcamo

Partinico

Piana
di Albanesi

Misilmeri

Marineo

SS 121

Trabia   Términi
Imerese   SS 113

A20

35

I dello Stagnone

A29

SS 115

Sálemi

52

SS 188

VAL   DI   MAZARA

San Cipirello

Cáccamo

Villafrati

1613
R BUSAMBRA   SS 121

Roccapalumbra
Ália   Caltavuturo

Buonfornello

SS 285

1979
PZO CARBONARA

Portolla Madonnuzza
1147

Collesano

Castelbuono

M
A
D
O
N
I
E

SS 286

Castellana

Petralia-
San Lucia

Portella
Gangi   SS 12

Marsala

SS 188   San Ninfa   SS 119

Gibellina

Partanna

63

Santa Margherita
di Belice

Corleone

SS 118

Prizzi   Lercara
Friddi

SS 118

68

S   I   C

Alimena

66   SS

TUNIS

Castelvetrano

SS 115   43

SS 188

Sambuca
di Sicília

M
O
N
T
I

Chiusa Scláfani

Bivona

SS 189

Vallelunga
Pratameno

SS 121

A19

Mazara del Vallo

A29

46   Lago
Aráncio

Caltabellotta

Menfi

SS 188

S
I
C
A
N
I

Búrgio

Alessándria
della Rocca

San Stéfano
Quisquina

Castéltérmini

Santa Caterina
Villarmosa   SS 121   30

Mussomeli

San Cataldo

Enna

Campobello
di Mazara

Marinella

C Granitola

C S Marco

Sciacca

Ribera   SS 118

San Biágio Plátani

Serradifalco

Caltanissetta

Pia
Arm

Aragona

SS 610   58

Canicatti   Délia

Pietraperzia

SS 191

Barrafranca

SS 190

Sommatino

Mazzar

2

Raffadali

SS 115   73   SS 118

SS 189

SS 122

SS 123

Favara   Naro

Campobello
di Licata

Riesi

V
A
L
L

Lago d

Agrigento

Porto Empedocle

SS 410   Palma di
Montechiaro   47

Ravanusa

Butera

SS 190

Licata   SS 115   34

SS 117

Gela

MEDITERRANEAN SEA

(MARE MEDITERRANO)

LINOSA
LAMPEDUSA

Isole di Pantelleria

1

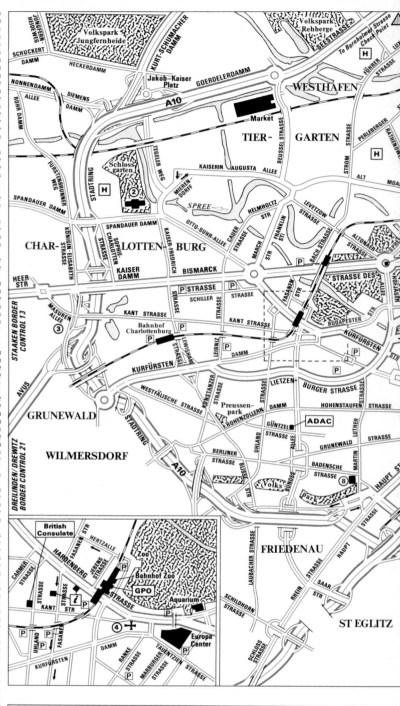

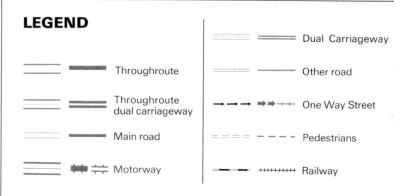

LEGEND

- Dual Carriageway
- Throughroute
- Other road
- Throughroute dual carriageway
- One Way Street
- Main road
- Pedestrians
- Motorway
- Railway

Austria

End of two-way traffic

Diversion

One-way street

Federal highway without priority

Federal highway with priority

Belgium

Restriction of traffic movement due to closing of anti-thaw barriers

Stopping or parking prohibited—on left on odd-numbered dates and on right on even-numbered dates

Beginning of Blue Zone parking area

Beginning of Blue Zone parking area

End of Blue Zone parking area

All traffic to move in parallel lanes. Number of arrows denotes number of lanes authorized

Denmark

Compulsory lane for lorries 0·2km ahead, lasting for 2·2km

Compulsory lane for lorries

Overtaking prohibited

Beginning of 1hr parking zone

End of 1hr parking zone

France, Andorra and Monaco

Yield to traffic from right

Crossroads protected by stop signs on side roads

Irregular stretch of road

Use of horn prohibited

Germany

Road with directions to motorways

Detour for vehicles over 5.5 metric tons

Road works: lane changes 1,000m ahead

Emergency motorway traffic diversion

No overtaking for lorries, coaches, and cars with caravans

European network road number

Road number

Italy and San Marino

No overtaking for vehicles towing trailers

End of restriction

Coaches have priority on mountain roads

Obligatory lane for slow commercial traffic

Left to right: overtaking lane, normal lane, and emergency lane

Wheel-chains, spiked or studded tyres, or snow tyres compulsory at 174km

Netherlands

Beginning of Blue Zone parking

End of Blue Zone parking

Danger-trams crossing

Front view of traffic pillar: motor vehicles may pass on either side; other traffic on right only

Cycle crossings

Spain

Turning permitted

No entry

Switzerland

Prohibition sign (showing exceptions)

Mountain postal coach route: coaches have priority

End of route

Exit road

Slow lane

Warning of road conditions on mountain passes:

eg pass closed; road open as far as Realp; wheel-chains, spiked, studded, or snow tyres compulsory

Göschenen – Andermatt open; Gotthard – wheel chains compulsory; Furka closed; Oberalp – wheel-chains, spiked, studded, or snow tyres compulsory

INTERNATIONAL ROAD SIGNS

DANGER WARNING SIGNS

The following symbols may also appear in a yellow square with one diagonal vertical instead of in a red triangle.

Right bend (left bend if the symbol is reversed) — Double bend, the first to the left (first bend to right if symbol reversed) — Dangerous bend

Dangerous descent — Steep ascent — Carriageway narrows — Carriageway narrows

Swing bridge — Road leads onto quay or river bank — Uneven road — Ridge

Dip — Slippery road — Loose gravel — Falling rocks

Pedestrian crossing — Children — Cyclists entering or crossing — Road works

Cattle or other animals crossing — Light signals

Airfield — Cross-wind — Two-way traffic — Other dangers

PRIORITY SIGNS ON NARROW ROADS

Oncoming traffic has priority — Priority over oncoming traffic

SIGNS AT ROAD JUNCTIONS

"Give way" sign

Advance warning of "give way" sign

200m

"Priority road" sign — "Stop" sign (New) — "End of priority" sign

Stop sign (Old)

SIGNS BEFORE ROAD JUNCTIONS

Intersection with a road the users of which must give way — Intersection where the priority is that prescribed by the general priority rule in force in the country — Roundabout

SIGNS AT LEVEL CROSSINGS

Level-crossing with gates or staggered half-gates — Other level-crossings — Intersection with a tramway line

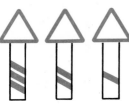

Signs placed in the immediate vicinity of level-crossings

Approaches to level-crossings

PROHIBITORY OR REGULATORY SIGNS

No entry — Closed to all vehicles in both directions — No entry for any power driven vehicle except two-wheeled motor cycles without side-car — No entry for motor cycles

No entry for cycles — No entry for mopeds — No entry for pedestrians — No entry for handcarts

No entry for any power driven vehicle drawing a trailer other than a semi-trailer or a single axle trailer — No entry for goods vehicles — No entry for vehicles carrying more than a certain quantity of explosives or readily inflammable substances — No entry for vehicles carrying more than a certain quantity of substances liable to cause water pollution

No entry for animal-drawn vehicles — No entry for power driven agricultural vehicles — No entry for power driven vehicles — No entry for power driven vehicles or animal-drawn vehicles